ASIA BOND MONITOR

JUNE 2025

ASIAN DEVELOPMENT BANK

ADB

6 ADB Avenue, Mandaluyong City, 1550 Metro Manila, Philippines
Tel +63 2 8632 4444; Fax +63 2 8636 2444
www.adb.org

ISBN 978-92-9277-340-3 (print); 978-92-9277-341-0 (PDF); 978-92-9277-342-7 (e-book)
ISSN 2219-1518 (print), 2219-1526 (PDF)
Publication Stock No. SGP250236-2
DOI: http://dx.doi.org/10.22617/SGP250236-2

Note:
ADB recognizes "China" as the People's Republic of China; "Hong Kong" as Hong Kong, China; "Korea" as the Republic of Korea; "Vietnam" as Viet Nam; and "Hanoi" as Ha Noi.

Cover design by Erickson Mercado.

Contents

Emerging East Asian Local Currency Bond Markets: A Regional Update

Executive Summary

Recent Developments in Financial Conditions in Emerging East Asia

Between 3 March and 30 May, financial conditions in emerging East Asia remained resilient amid heightened global uncertainty and the prospect of a higher-for-longer monetary stance from the United States (US) Federal Reserve.[1] Investor sentiment weakened in March–April over trade policy uncertainty but recovered in May following progress in trade negotiations between the US and its trading partners, especially the People's Republic of China (PRC).

During the review period, financial markets posted mixed patterns. Risk premiums, proxied by credit default swap spreads, marginally widened by 1.6 basis points (simple average) and 3.5 basis points (gross-domestic-product-weighted average), and foreign investors withdrew USD27.1 billion from the region's equity markets. At the same time, equity markets gained 2.0% (simple average) and 1.6% (market-weighted average), supported by improved sentiment, particularly in May. Meanwhile, uncertainty over economic policies, rising debt levels, and a worsening fiscal position dampened investor confidence in USD-denominated assets, leading to a broad strengthening of regional currencies. Regional currencies appreciated 2.3% (simple average) and 1.7% (gross-domestic-product-weighted average) against the US dollar during the review period. Across the region, continued monetary easing and disinflation contributed to inflows in local currency (LCY) bond markets and declining bond yields.

Risks to regional financial conditions remain tilted to the downside. While trade tensions between the PRC and the US have eased for the time being, uncertainty over trade policies remains. The possible further escalation in trade tensions could delay investments, disrupt supply chains, stifle cross-border capital flows, reignite inflation, and increase market volatility. Heightened uncertainty and higher-for-longer interest rates in the US could also slow regional monetary easing, increasing the debt burdens of borrowers and weakening their balance sheets. Other downside risks include the possibility of wider conflict in the Middle East, which could increase food and energy prices and add to global uncertainty. Within the region, the PRC's property sector remains vulnerable and uncertainty over its possible further deterioration might weaken consumer and business sentiment and depress economic activity. In the medium term, extreme weather events could also negatively impact growth and inflation.

Recent Developments in Local Currency Bond Markets in Emerging East Asia

The emerging East Asian LCY bond market totaled USD27.2 trillion at the end of March, with growth easing to 2.7% quarter-on-quarter (q-o-q) in the first quarter (Q1) of 2025 from 3.1% q-o-q in the fourth quarter (Q4) of 2024 amid elevated global uncertainty. LCY government bonds outstanding (USD17.5 trillion) grew 3.8% q-o-q in Q1 2025, down from 4.0% q-o-q in the prior quarter, as a large volume of maturities in the PRC capped the regional market's overall expansion. Corporate bonds outstanding (USD9.0 trillion) rose 1.0% q-o-q in Q1 2025, compared with 1.6% q-o-q growth in the previous quarter, as private sector bond issuance contracted. The total bond stock of members of the Association of Southeast Asian Nations (ASEAN) expanded 2.2% q-o-q to USD2.5 trillion and accounted for 9.1% of the emerging East Asian total at the end of March. Growth in ASEAN LCY bond markets in Q1 2025 was supported by robust issuance of sovereign bonds as most governments front-loaded their annual borrowing. At the end of Q1 2025, 55.6% of outstanding Treasury bonds in the region had remaining tenors of over 5 years, with a size-weighted average tenor of 8.4 years. Banks and insurance and pension funds were the top two holders of outstanding Treasury bonds in emerging East Asia at the end of March, holding an average of 34.8% and 29.2% of the existing debt stock, respectively.

[1] Emerging East Asia is defined to include member states of the Association of Southeast Asian Nations plus the People's Republic of China; Hong Kong, China; and the Republic of Korea.

LCY bond issuance in the region contracted 0.5% q-o-q to USD2.6 trillion in Q1 2025, after declining 7.4% q-o-q in Q4 2024, driven by reduced corporate bond issuance. Private sector bond issuance fell 12.1% q-o-q on weak investor appetite amid ongoing global trade tensions. Meanwhile, issuance of government bonds in emerging East Asia rose 8.1% q-o-q, with nearly all markets registering higher issuance volumes in Q1 2025 than in the previous quarter, in line with regional governments' front-loading practices at the start of the year. The Government of the PRC drove the growth in regional government bond issuance as it financed stimulus measures to support the domestic economy. Aggregate LCY bond issuance in ASEAN markets amounted to USD0.6 trillion in Q1 2025, representing 24.2% of the regional total, up from 23.3% in Q4 2024.

Recent Developments in ASEAN+3 Sustainable Bond Markets

Sustainable bonds outstanding in ASEAN+3 markets reached USD922.7 billion at the end of March, with growth decelerating to 0.3% q-o-q in Q1 2025 from 2.9% q-o-q in Q4 2024.[2] The moderating expansion was driven by dampened investor appetite amid heightened global market uncertainties. ASEAN+3 accounted for 18.3% of the global sustainable bond stock at the end of March as the world's second-largest regional market, trailing only the European Union 20 (36.6%). The sustainable bond market of ASEAN+3, however, accounted for only 2.3% of its general bond market, compared with the corresponding share of 8.3% in the European Union 20. Meanwhile, aggregate sustainable bonds outstanding in ASEAN markets tallied USD96.1 billion at the end of March, accounting for 10.4% of the total ASEAN+3 sustainable bond stock, compared with ASEAN's share of only 6.0% of bonds outstanding in the ASEAN+3 general bond market.

Sustainable bond issuance in ASEAN+3 totaled USD47.7 billion in Q1 2025, posting a 24.0% q-o-q contraction on heightened global uncertainty. Over half (55.2%) of ASEAN+3 sustainable bond issuance in Q1 2025 was from the PRC. ASEAN markets collectively accounted for 9.0% of ASEAN+3's sustainable bond issuance, while leading the region's issuance of sustainability bonds in Q1 2025 with a 36.5% share. ASEAN+3 saw less LCY and long-term financing in sustainable bond markets in Q1 2025 compared with 2024. The LCY financing share of ASEAN+3 sustainable bond issuance ticked down to 72.9% in Q1 2025 from 75.8% in full-year 2024. Only 16.6% of sustainable bond issuances carried maturities of more than 5 years in Q1 2025, compared with 26.5% in 2024. As a result, the size-weighted average maturity of ASEAN+3 sustainable bond issuance fell to 5.1 years in Q1 2025 from 6.0 years in 2024. ASEAN economies had a higher share of long-term financing in Q1 2025 than the ASEAN+3 average due to relatively more public sector issuance: 59.9% of sustainable bond issuance in ASEAN markets carried maturities of over 5 years, with a size-weighted average tenor of 10.2 years.

2 ASEAN+3 comprises the member states of the Association of Southeast Asian Nations (ASEAN) plus the People's Republic of China; Hong Kong, China; Japan; and the Republic of Korea.

Developments in Regional Financial Conditions

Emerging East Asian financial conditions remained resilient amid heightened global uncertainty between 3 March and 30 May.[1] Intensified trade tensions and uncertainty surrounding negotiations between the United States (US) and its trading partners raised investor risk aversion and clouded the global economic outlook, especially in March and April. In May, improvements in financial conditions were observed following trade negotiations between the US and some of its trading partners, particularly the People's Republic of China (PRC). During the review period, mixed patterns were observed in regional financial markets. Risk premiums marginally widened and net equity portfolio outflows were recorded, while optimism over trade negotiations and various domestic factors supported regional equity markets, especially in May. Meanwhile, regional currencies strengthened against the US dollar due to weakened investor confidence in USD-denominated assets over uncertainty in US economic policies, a widening federal budget deficit and elevated debt levels, and the downgrade of the US' sovereign credit rating. Continued monetary easing and disinflation contributed to the decline in both short- and long-term bond yields in most regional bond markets (**Table A**). Nevertheless, uncertainty still clouds the outlook for regional financial conditions pending the outcome of trade negotiations, especially given that the current pause on US tariff implementation expires in July.

During the review period, 10-year bond yields rose in the US, driven by several factors. First, the Federal Reserve (Fed) maintained its higher-for-longer monetary stance, citing the resilient US economic performance and uncertainty about the possible inflationary impact of tariffs. Moreover, subdued investor confidence in USD-denominated assets led to sales of US Treasuries, pushing up US bond yields. Aside from uncertainty over US economic policies, there were also concerns that the federal budget deficit would worsen. On 16 May, Moody's

Table A: Changes in Financial Conditions in Major Advanced Economies and Select Emerging East Asian Markets from 3 March 2025 to 30 May 2025

	2-Year Government Bond Yield (bps)	10-Year Government Bond Yield (bps)	5-Year Credit Default Swap Spread (bps)	Equity Index (%)	FX Rate (%)
Major Advanced Economies					
Euro Area	(29)	0.9	–	(3.1)	8.2
Japan	(9)	9	5.6	3.0	3.8
United States	(5)	25	–	1.1	–
Select Emerging East Asian Markets					
People's Republic of China	8	(6)	4.2	0.9	1.2
Hong Kong, China	(139)	(56)	–	1.2	(0.8)
Indonesia	(25)	(5)	1.6	10.1	1.2
Republic of Korea	(32)	7	(0.1)	6.5	5.6
Malaysia	(31)	(26)	2.8	(4.0)	4.9
Philippines	(11)	15	(7.3)	5.0	3.8
Singapore	(61)	(30)	–	(0.4)	4.3
Thailand	(35)	(36)	5.8	(3.3)	4.1
Viet Nam	5	3	4.2	1.8	(1.6)

( ) = negative, – = not available, bps = basis points, FX = foreign exchange.

Note: FX rates are presented against the United States dollar. A positive (negative) value for the FX rate indicates the appreciation (depreciation) of the local currency against the United States dollar.

Source: *AsianBondsOnline* calculations based on Bloomberg LP data.

[1] Emerging East Asia is defined to include member states of the Association of Southeast Asian Nations plus the People's Republic of China; Hong Kong, China; and the Republic of Korea.

downgraded the US' sovereign credit rating from Aaa to Aa1, citing the worsening fiscal deficit as well as a significant build-up of debt. Following the downgrade, the US has now lost its AAA rating from all three major rating agencies. On 22 May, the US House of Representatives passed a new tax and spending bill. The provisions of the bill expand and extend previous tax cuts and add new tax deductions such as for car loans and tips. Market concerns of higher debt levels and a worsening fiscal position thus led to a surge of 12 basis points (bps) for 10-year US bond yields between 16 May and 21 May. US Treasury yields fell slightly on 23 May, following Treasury Secretary Scott Bessent's announcement that the government was considering scrapping a regulation that limits banks' ability to hold Treasury bonds. Meanwhile, the 2-year bond yield declined during the review period. The decline mostly occurred in March and April, driven by expectations of a bigger cumulative rate cut in 2025 than the Fed's December 2024 projection of 50 bps (**Figure A**). The 2-year bond yield rose in May after the Fed reaffirmed the prospect of a higher-for-longer monetary stance.

The US economy remains resilient, but recent economic data show some signs of weakening. Gross domestic product (GDP) in the US contracted an annualized 0.2% in the first quarter (Q1) of 2025 after gaining 2.4% in the fourth quarter (Q4) of 2024, largely due to a surge in imports ahead of the full implementation of tariffs, which widened the trade deficit; a slowdown in domestic consumption to 1.2% in Q1 2025 from 4.0% in Q4 2024; and a 0.7% contraction in government expenditures in Q1 2025 versus an expansion of 3.1% in Q4 2024. Retail sales remained subdued. Growth softened to 0.1% month-on-month (m-o-m) in April from 1.7% m-o-m in March, due to weak consumer demand and a high base effect from front-loaded purchases before the full implementation of tariffs, but was still higher than February's 0.0% growth. The S&P Global US Manufacturing Purchasing Managers Index (PMI) recovered in May, rising to 52.0 from 50.2 in both April and March. Industrial production was unchanged on a monthly basis in April after contracting 0.3% m-o-m in March. Consumer confidence rose to 98.0 in May from 85.7 in April and 93.9 in March, but still lower than that of February (100.1) and January (105.3). Nevertheless, the US labor market remained solid. Nonfarm payroll additions recorded 139,000 in May, slightly down from 147,000 in April, but up from 120,000 in March and 102,000 in February. The unemployment rate held steady at 4.2% in May, April and March, which was slightly higher than February's 4.1%. The generally weak economic data echoed the Fed's projections in March, when it revised downward its 2025 GDP growth forecast to 1.7% from a December estimate of 2.1% and revised upward its 2025 unemployment rate forecast to 4.4% from a December estimate of 4.3%.

Inflation in the US continued to soften during the review period yet remained above the Fed's 2.0% target. In April, consumer price inflation eased to 2.3% year-on-year (y-o-y) from 2.4% y-o-y in March, 2.8% y-o-y in February, and 3.0% y-o-y in January. Personal Consumption Expenditure (PCE) inflation fell to 2.1% y-o-y in April from 2.3% y-o-y in March and 2.6% y-o-y in February. Core PCE inflation slowed to 2.5% y-o-y in April from 2.7% y-o-y in March and 2.9% y-o-y in February. Nevertheless, the Fed raised the inflation forecast during its March meeting because of the possible inflationary impact of tariffs. The PCE inflation forecast for full-year 2025 was raised to 2.7% from 2.5% in December, while the core PCE inflation forecast for full-year 2025 was raised to 2.8% from 2.5%.

Heightened uncertainty contributed to the higher-for-longer monetary stance in the US. During its March and May Federal Open Market Committee (FOMC) meetings, the Fed left the federal funds target rate range unchanged at 4.25%–4.50% and maintained its December 2024 forecast of a cumulative 50 bps rate cut in 2025. However, in March, the individual forecasts of Fed members turned slightly hawkish compared to December, while the Fed highlighted that the economy risked higher inflation and unemployment amid rising uncertainty. On 7 May, Fed Chair Jerome Powell discussed the ongoing uncertainties surrounding tariffs, citing that such policies are still evolving, making their impacts on the economy unclear. Thus, the Fed indicated a wait-and-see attitude, which raised the likelihood of a higher-for-longer monetary stance given the Fed's assessment of a resilient economic outlook.[2] Prior to the 6–7 May FOMC meeting, concerns regarding US tariffs and a possible economic slowdown had driven up the combined probability of a 75 bps (36.4%) or 100 bps (28.9%) cumulative rate cut in 2025 to 65.2%, while the expected chance of either a 25 bps (5.4%) or 50 bps (20.7%) cumulative rate cut had fallen to 26.1% (Figure A). However, after the May FOMC meeting, market expectations that the Fed would

[2] Some Fed officials similarly highlighted the need for caution. For example, on 27 March, Fed Bank of Richmond President Tom Barkin said that a moderately restrictive monetary policy is appropriate in the face of rapid changes in US economic policy. On 11 April, Fed Bank of New York President John Williams said that he expects tariffs to raise inflation but that it is also hard to assess the overall impact of policy changes on the economy. On 22 April, Fed Governor Adriana Kugler said that given the tariffs' inflationary pressures, it was best to maintain the Fed's current policy rate.

Figure A: Daily Probability of Cumulative Rate Adjustments by the Federal Reserve in 2025

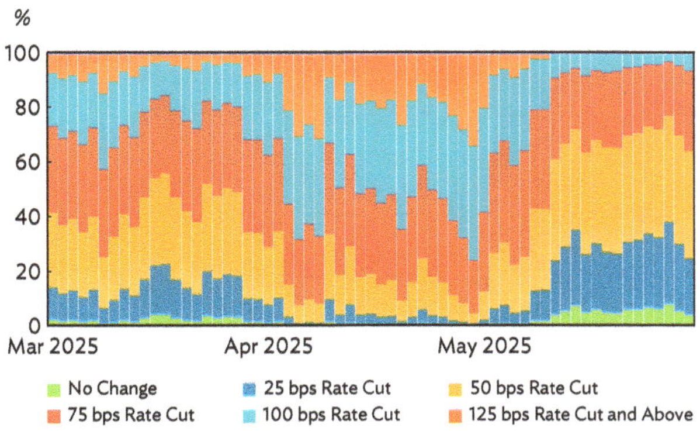

bps = basis points.
Note: Data are as of 30 May 2025.
Source: CME FedWatch Tool.

hold a higher-for-longer policy stance increased, with the combined chance of a 25 bps or 50 bps cumulative rate cut in 2025 immediately rising to 41.1% on 8 May and further to 60.3% by 30 May, with the chance of either a 75 bps or 100 bps cumulative rate cut declining to 35.8%.

In the euro area, the 2-year yield declined between 3 March and 30 May on continued disinflation and monetary easing by the European Central Bank (ECB). However, the 10-year yield rose over expectations of widening budget deficits driven by increased defense and infrastructure spending following comments from US officials that North Atlantic Treaty Organization members needed to increase defense spending as a percentage of GDP. The euro area's economy has remained resilient. GDP grew 1.5% y-o-y in Q1 2025 from 1.2% y-o-y in Q4 2024, while GDP growth also accelerated on a quarter-on-quarter basis to 0.6% in Q1 2025 from 0.3% in the prior quarter. The manufacturing PMI remained in contraction but continued to trend upward, rising to 49.4 in May from 49.0 in April and 48.6 in March. Nevertheless, heightened global uncertainties also dampened the euro area's growth outlook. In March, the ECB updated its GDP growth forecast by revising downward its projections for full-year 2025 and 2026 to 0.9% and 1.2%, respectively, from December forecasts of 1.1% and 1.4%. Annual inflation in the euro area also continued to trend downward, falling to 1.9% in May from 2.2% each in April and March, and 2.3% in February. However, in its March forecast, the ECB raised its full-year 2025 inflation projection to 2.3% from 2.1% in December and kept its 2026 forecast unchanged at 1.9%. In its June update, the ECB left unchanged the 2025 GDP growth forecast at 0.9% but revised downward the 2026 forecast to 1.1%. In addition, the ECB reduced its 2025 and 2026 inflation projections to 2.0% and 1.6%, respectively.

The ECB continued to ease monetary policy over moderating inflation, while remaining cautious amid rising uncertainty. The ECB reduced its key policy rates by 25 bps each at its 6 March and 17 April meetings. The ECB noted that the disinflation process remained on track. However, during its April meeting, the ECB mentioned that the outlook had deteriorated over rising trade uncertainty. While many ECB members are in favor of further rate cuts, some have expressed caution. For example, on 22 April, ECB President Christine Lagarde said that the disinflation process was almost done and that they must remain data dependent to properly assess the impact of US trade policies. On 28 April, Bank of Ireland Governor Gabriel Makhlouf advocated for caution, saying he favored a meeting-by-meeting approach due to uncertainty about inflation over the medium-term. On 5 May, Bank of Greece Governor Yannis Stournaras said that the ECB is set to continue cutting interest rates but also expressed caution. Amid ongoing global uncertainty, the ECB reduced policy rates by 25 bps on 5 June, citing the ongoing disinflation process and need to support growth.

Bond yields in Japan fell at the short-end of the curve between 3 March and 30 May over an expected softening in the Bank of Japan's (BOJ) monetary stance and continued disinflation. However, tariff-related concerns led to speculation that Japan would pass a supplemental budget to aid the economy. There were also concerns about the government's fiscal position following a proposal for consumption tax cuts ahead of upcoming elections. The Japanese government has since pushed back on the idea of implementing such cuts. In addition, yields faced upward pressure following the reduction of Japanese government bond investments by four major insurance companies because of high volatility and low liquidity, pushing up long-term bond yields during the review period. In contrast to the easing monetary stances of both the Fed and the ECB, the BOJ previously adopted a tightening stance, raising the policy rate in its January meeting. However, with heightened uncertainty in the

[3] For example, on 24 April, Banque de France Governor Francois Villeroy de Galhau said that the expected decline in inflation warranted further rate cuts. On 26 April, Bank of Lithuania Governor Gediminas Simkus said that he saw two more rate cuts this year. On 28 April, Bank of Finland Governor Olli Rehn said that it was possible for inflation to fall further than expected and that this would allow for further rate cuts.

global trade environment, the BOJ left the policy rate unchanged at its 19 March meeting, noting that the high level of uncertainty surrounding trade policies could affect the paths of inflation and growth. On 16 April, BOJ Governor Kazuo Ueda said that the central bank may need to take action if US tariffs impact Japan's growth, hinting at a continuation of the pause in rate hikes at the monetary policy meeting in May. As expected, the BOJ held the policy rate steady at its 1 May meeting. The Japanese economy remains largely subdued, with annualized GDP contracting 0.2% in Q1 2025—following annualized growth of 2.2% in Q4 2024 and 0.9% in the third quarter of 2024—over a decline in exports and weak consumption. The manufacturing PMI continued in a contractionary regime, with a May reading of 49.4, slightly higher than April's and March's readings of 48.7 and 48.4, respectively. The unemployment rate remained at 2.5% in March and April, but slightly higher than 2.4% in February. Meanwhile, disinflation continued, with inflation falling to 3.6% y-o-y in April and March from 3.7% y-o-y in February and 4.0% y-o-y in January, although it remained above the BOJ's 2.0% target. In light of heightened trade uncertainty, in May the BOJ revised downward its full-year 2025 and 2026 GDP growth projections to 0.5% and 0.7%, respectively, from projections of 1.1% and 1.0% made in January. The BOJ also reduced its full-year 2025 and 2026 inflation forecasts to 2.2% and 1.7%, respectively, from January projections of 2.4% and 2.0%.

Continued disinflation and monetary easing, combined with the moderated growth outlook over mounting global trade uncertainties, contributed to a decline in LCY government bond yields in most emerging East Asian economies during the review period (**Table B**). Ongoing monetary easing was supported by continued disinflation in the region (**Figure B**). Inflation saw a rise only in Hong Kong, China, over faster increases in housing and transport costs, and in Indonesia, where inflation rose on higher housing and food prices but remained within the central bank's target range. Yields for 2-year and 10-year bonds declined the most in Hong Kong, China as the Hong Kong Monetary Authority expanded the money supply by selling Hong Kong dollars to maintain the dollar peg following the overall appreciation of regional currencies against the US dollar. The next largest decline in yields during the review period was seen in Singapore, largely driven by two consecutive easing adjustments, in January and April, by the Monetary Authority of Singapore to the Singapore dollar nominal effective exchange rate, in line with a lower inflation forecast and a weakened economic outlook. The Bank of Thailand eased monetary policy via consecutive rate cuts in February and April, as the central bank assessed that the Thai economy was likely to slow and inflation to further moderate. The Bangko Sentral ng Pilipinas reduced its policy rate by 25 bps on 10 April amid lower inflation and noted that

Table B: Changes in Monetary Stances in Major Advanced Economies and Select Emerging East Asian Markets

Economy	Policy Rate 1-May-2024 (%)	Rate Change (%) May-2024	Jun-2024	Jul-2024	Aug-2024	Sep-2024	Oct-2024	Nov-2024	Dec-2024	Jan-2025	Feb-2025	Mar-2025	Apr-2025	May-2025	Policy Rate 30-May-2025 (%)	Change in Policy Rates (basis points)
Euro Area	4.00		↓0.25			↓0.25	↓0.25		↓0.25		↓0.25	↓0.25	↓0.25		2.25	↓ 175
Japan	0.10			↑0.15						↑0.25					0.50	↑ 40
United Kingdom	5.25				↓0.25			↓0.25			↓0.25			↓0.25	4.25	↓ 100
United States	5.50					↓0.50		↓0.25	↓0.25						4.50	↓ 100
People's Republic of China	1.80			↓0.10		↓0.20								↓0.10	1.40	↓ 40
Indonesia	6.25					↓0.25				↓0.25				↓0.25	5.50	↓ 75
Republic of Korea	3.50						↓0.25	↓0.25			↓0.25			↓0.25	2.50	↓ 100
Malaysia	3.00														3.00	◆ 0
Philippines	6.50				↓0.25		↓0.25		↓0.25				↓0.25		5.50	↓ 100
Singapore	–									↓			↓		–	↓ –
Thailand	2.50						↓0.25				↓0.25		↓0.25		1.75	↓ 75
Viet Nam	4.50														4.50	◆ 0

( ) = negative, ◆ = no change, – = no data.

Notes:
1. Data coverage is from 1 May 2024 to 30 May 2025.
2. For the People's Republic of China, data used in the chart is for the 7-day reverse repurchase rate.
3. For the United States, the upper bound of the policy rate target range is reported on the table.
4. The up (down) arrow for Singapore signifies monetary policy tightening (loosening) by its central bank. The Monetary Authority of Singapore utilizes the Singapore dollar nominal effective exchange rate to guide its monetary policy.

Sources: Various central bank websites.

Figure B: Inflation in Major Advanced Economies and Select Emerging East Asian Markets

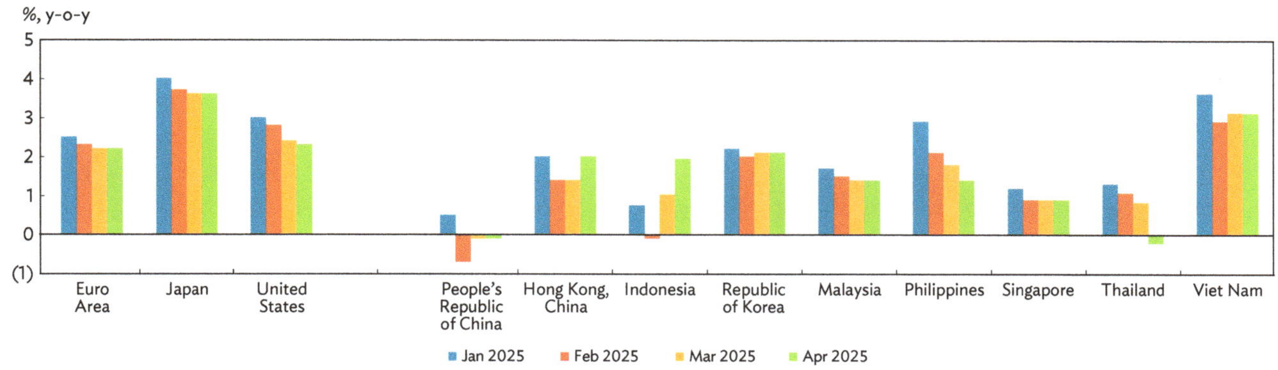

( ) = negative, y-o-y = year-on-year.
Sources: Various local sources.

the external outlook for the Philippines has become challenging. Bank Indonesia and the Bank of Korea each lowered their policy rate by another 25 bps on 21 May and 29 May, respectively, following their 25 bps rate cuts in January and February, to support economic growth amid heightened uncertainty over trade policies. The People's Bank of China announced easing measures in response to trade uncertainty by cutting the 7-day reverse repo rate by 10 bps on 6 May and the 1-year and 5-year loan prime rates by 10 bps each on 20 May. The People's Bank of China also reduced the reserve requirement ratio by 50 bps on 15 May. Similarly, on 8 May, Bank Negara Malaysia lowered the statutory reserve requirement ratio by 100 bps to 1.0% to support the financial market amid ongoing uncertainties.

Table C: Gross Domestic Product Growth in Select Emerging East Asian Economies (y-o-y, %)

	2024		2025	Forecast for
Economy	Q3	Q4	Q1	2025
PRC	4.60	5.40	5.40	4.70
HKG	1.90	2.50	3.10	2.30
INO	4.95	5.02	4.87	5.00
ROK	1.50	1.10	0.00	1.50
MAL	5.40	4.90	4.40	4.90
PHI	5.24	5.30	5.40	6.00
SIN	5.70	5.00	3.90	2.60
THA	3.00	3.30	3.10	2.80
VIE	7.43	7.55	6.93	6.60

PRC = People's Republic of China; HKG = Hong Kong, China; INO = Indonesia; ROK = Republic of Korea; MAL = Malaysia; PHI = Philippines; Q1 = first quarter; Q3 = third quarter; Q4 = fourth quarter; SIN = Singapore; THA = Thailand; VIE = Viet Nam; y-o-y = year-on-year.
Note: Forecasts for 2025 are based on the *Asian Development Outlook April 2025*.
Sources: Various local sources.

Economic performance moderated in Q1 2025 in most regional markets. GDP growth in Singapore decelerated to 3.9% y-o-y from 5.0% y-o-y in Q4 2024 amid a slowdown in the manufacturing, trade, and service sectors (**Table C**). A slower pace of economic expansion was also noted in Malaysia—with growth dragged down by a slowdown in the construction, service, and manufacturing sectors—and in Viet Nam, as growth in the industrial and service sectors decelerated. In the Republic of Korea, GDP was unchanged in Q1 2025, following growth of 1.1% y-o-y in Q4 2024, over lingering political concerns as well as a worsening trade outlook. On the other hand, in Hong Kong, China, economic growth accelerated to 3.1% y-o-y in Q1 2025 from 2.5% y-o-y in Q4 2024, buoyed by strong exports (8.7% y-o-y), imports (7.4% y-o-y), and a recovery in investments (2.8% y-o-y). GDP growth in the Philippines also accelerated to 5.4% y-o-y in Q1 2025, up from 5.3% y-o-y growth in the previous quarter, over increased consumption and government spending. The April 2025 edition of the *Asian Development Outlook* forecast slightly weaker economic growth in 2025 of 4.4% for East Asia, down from 4.7% in 2024, largely due to continued weakness in the PRC's property sector and increased tariffs. The growth forecast in Southeast Asia also reflected marginal weakening to 4.7% in 2025 from 4.8% in 2024, driven by a slowdown in the oil and gas sector in Brunei Darussalam and slowing export growth in Malaysia, Singapore, and Viet Nam.

Uncertainty over US trade policies and their potential impacts on US economic performance, combined with a high level of debt and large fiscal deficit, have generated investor risk aversion toward USD-denominated assets, contributing to an overall strengthening of emerging East Asian currencies against the US dollar. From 3 March to 30 May, regional currencies appreciated 2.3% (simple average) and 1.7% (GDP-weighted average) against the US dollar. Among all regional currencies, the Korean won and Malaysian ringgit appreciated the most at 5.6% and 4.9%, respectively (Table A, **Figure C**). The Korean won was aided by a number of favorable factors: news of trade negotiations between the Republic of Korea and the US, improving sentiment in the semiconductor sector following the announcement of a supply deal between Saudi Arabia and Nvidia, as well as the announcement of snap elections that pared ongoing political concerns. The Malaysian ringgit was supported by an influx of foreign funds into its bond market. In contrast, the Vietnamese dong weakened the most among all regional currencies during the review period, dipping 1.6% versus the dollar, largely driven by dampened sentiment in the manufacturing sector, as its manufacturing PMI dropped to 45.6 in April from 50.5 in March amid trade policy uncertainty. In May, the manufacturing PMI rose to 49.8.

Figure C: Currency Exchange Rates Against the United States Dollar in Select Emerging East Asian Markets

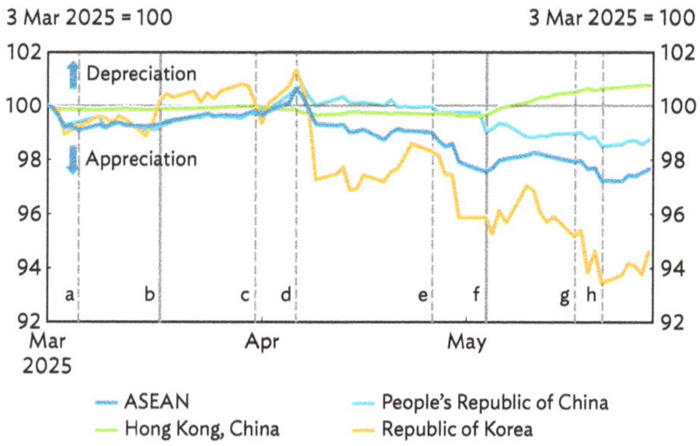

ASEAN = Association of Southeast Asian Nations.

Notes:

1. Corresponding dates of the following events:
   a Fed Chair Jerome Powell signals a slower pace of rate cuts in 2025 amid heightened uncertainty in the United States' (US) economic outlook.
   b The Fed maintains the federal funds rate at a range of 4.25%–4.50% and keeps its projection for two rate cuts in 2025.
   c "Reciprocal tariff" policy of the US with its trading partner economies takes effect.
   d US President Donald Trump announces a 90-day pause on reciprocal tariffs, except for those on the People's Republic of China.
   e US President Donald Trump signs an executive order easing some tariff measures.
   f The Fed maintains the federal funds rate at a range of 4.25%–4.50% amid elevated inflation and increased economic uncertainty.
   g Moody's downgrades the US sovereign credit rating from Aaa to Aa1, adding to investor concerns.
   h US President Donald Trump imposes 50% tariffs on all European Union imports to the US starting 1 June.
2. ASEAN comprises the markets of Brunei Darussalam, Cambodia, Indonesia, the Lao People's Democratic Republic, Malaysia, the Philippines, Singapore, Thailand, and Viet Nam.
3. Data are as of 30 May 2025.
4. An increase (decrease) in the value indicates depreciation (appreciation) of the currency against the US dollar.

Source: *AsianBondsOnline* calculations based on Bloomberg LP data.

Global uncertainty over trade policies have generated investor risk aversion, leading to the widening of risk premiums across the region. Credit default swap spreads, a proxy of risk premiums, marginally widened by 1.6 bps (simple average) and 3.5 bps (GDP-weighted average) during the review period. Nearly all regional markets recorded a widening of credit default swap spreads in March and April on mounting trade-related uncertainty (**Figure D**). In May, risk premiums collectively narrowed over expectations of progress in trade negotiations between the US and its trading partners, especially the PRC. On 12 May, the PRC and the US jointly announced an agreement based on their meeting in Geneva. Under the terms of the agreement, both governments agreed to reduce additional tariffs on each other to 10% for a 90-day period.

Subdued investor sentiment led to a similar pattern of portfolio outflows from regional equity markets. Between 3 March and 30 May, regional equity markets recorded net portfolio outflows of USD27.1 billion. Outflows were mainly observed in March–April, while net inflows of USD1.3 billion were recorded in regional markets in May over optimism on a deal between the PRC and the US to lower tariffs (**Figure E**). The Republic of Korea recorded large outflows in April over lingering domestic political issues alongside heightened trade uncertainty. ASEAN collectively posted net portfolio outflows of USD3.7 billion during the review period. The PRC recorded large outflows in March on the weakened domestic economic outlook and escalated trade tensions with the US. Outflows from the PRC's equity market continued in April but the outflows were smaller than

Figure D: Changes in Credit Default Swap Spreads in Select Emerging East Asian Markets (senior 5-year)

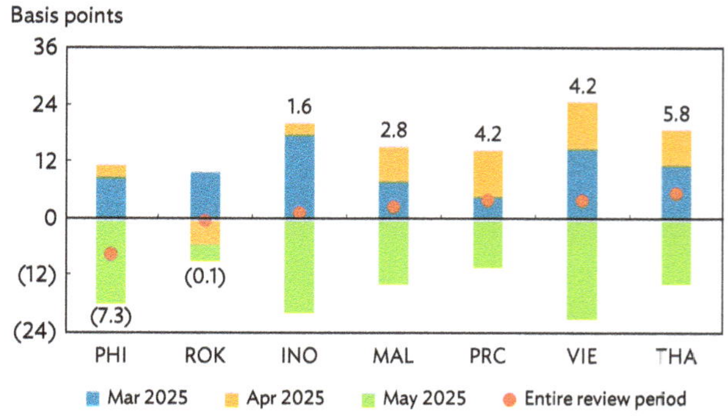

( ) = negative; PRC = People's Republic of China; INO = Indonesia; ROK = Republic of Korea; MAL = Malaysia; PHI = Philippines; THA = Thailand; VIE = Viet Nam.

Note: The numbers above (below) each bar refer to the change in spreads between 3 March 2025 and 30 May 2025.

Source: *AsianBondsOnline* calculations based on Bloomberg LP data.

Figure E: Foreign Capital Flows in Select Emerging East Asian Equity Markets

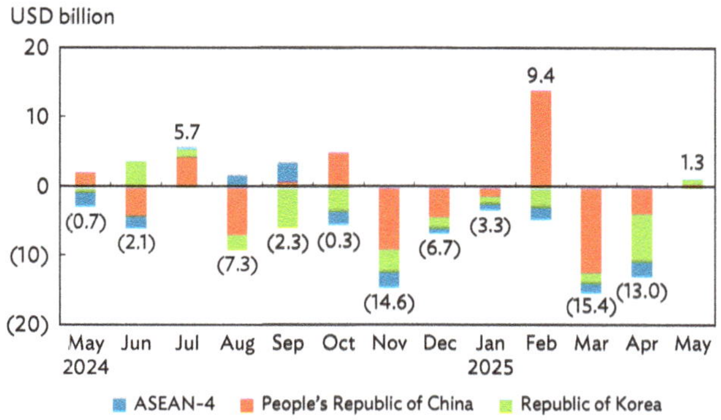

( ) = outflows, USD = United States dollar.

Notes:

1. Data coverage is from 1 May 2024 to 30 May 2025 except for Thailand (29 May 2025).
2. The numbers above (below) each bar refer to net inflows (net outflows) for each month.
3. Emerging East Asia is defined to include member states of the Association of Southeast Asian Nations plus the People's Republic of China; Hong Kong, China; and the Republic of Korea.
4. ASEAN-4 includes Indonesia, the Philippines, Thailand, and Viet Nam.

Source: Institute of International Finance.

Figure F: Foreign Capital Flows in Select Emerging East Asian Local Currency Bond Markets

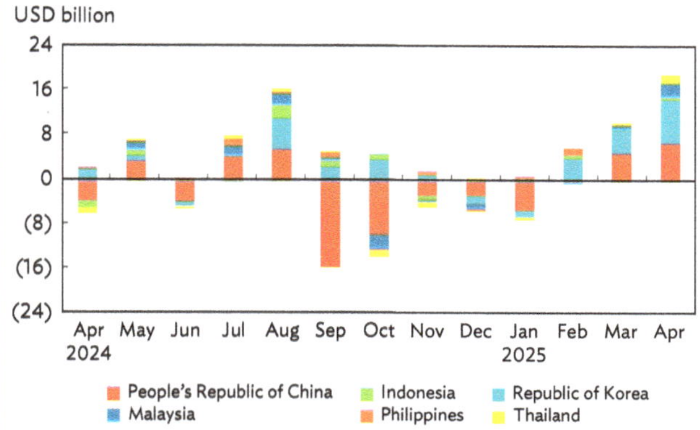

( ) = outflows, USD = United States dollar.

Notes:

1. The Republic of Korea and Thailand provided data on bond flows. For the People's Republic of China, Indonesia, Malaysia, and the Philippines, month-on-month changes in foreign holdings of local currency government bonds were used as a proxy for bond flows.
2. Data are as of 30 April 2025.
3. Figures were computed based on 30 April 2025 exchange rates and do not include currency effects.

Sources: People's Republic of China (Bloomberg LP); Indonesia (Directorate General of Budget Financing and Risk Management, Ministry of Finance); Republic of Korea (Financial Supervisory Service); Malaysia (Bank Negara Malaysia); Philippines (Bureau of the Treasury); and Thailand (Thai Bond Market Association).

in March due to increased expectations for a trade deal between the PRC and the US. In May, the PRC recorded portfolio inflows of USD0.5 billion.

Expectations of continued monetary easing and rising risk aversion in equity markets supported demand for regional bonds, as evidenced by capital inflows into the region's bond markets. Despite regional central banks expressing caution, expectations of the continuation of accommodative monetary stances in the region, or lower future interest rates, pushed up bond prices and attracted more investment. Most major bond markets in emerging East Asia recorded net capital inflows, driven by monetary easing among the region's central banks, leading to total net inflows of USD29.8 billion in March and April (**Figure F**). During the review period, the largest inflows in the region's LCY bond markets were recorded in the Republic of Korea, with USD12.0 billion in net capital inflows into its bond market following a rate cut in February and expectations of further easing to support economic growth amid rising uncertainty. Similarly, the PRC posted substantial inflows of USD11.8 billion amid the People's Bank of China's accommodative monetary policy stance in support of growth.

Recent optimism about trade negotiations between the US and its trade partners, as well as domestic factors, supported regional equity markets. The region's equity markets gained 2.0% (simple-average) and 1.6% (market-weighted average) from 3 March to 30 May. Five of nine regional equity markets declined in March due to various domestic factors (e.g., equity market losses in Malaysia were partly driven by declining palm oil prices). Most regional equity markets recorded equity losses in April too, due to intensified trade uncertainty, but expectations of progress in trade negotiations, particularly the trade deal between the PRC and the US, supported regional equity markets in May (**Figure G**). Indonesia's equity market gained the most during the review period, rising 10.1% on improved investor sentiment, especially over the news that the state social security fund would increase its equity portfolio allocation to 20% from 10% in the next 3 years. During the review period, equity markets in the Republic of Korea rose 6.5% over expectations of possible stock market reforms and further central bank rate cuts, and the Philippines' market gained 5.0% as it posted one of the highest GDP growth rates in the region as well as on expectations of increased domestic consumption resulting from election spending.

The risks to financial conditions highlighted in the March 2025 edition of the *Asia Bond Monitor* remain relevant, with risks continuing to skew to the downside. This is largely due to heightened uncertainty surrounding US trade policies and the expected higher-for-longer interest

Figure G: Changes in Equity Indexes in Select Emerging East Asian Markets

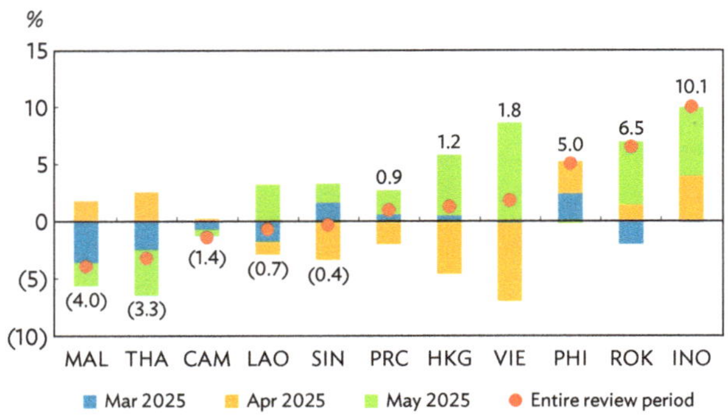

( ) = negative; CAM = Cambodia; PRC = People's Republic of China; HKG = Hong Kong, China; INO = Indonesia; ROK = Republic of Korea; LAO = Lao People's Democratic Republic; MAL = Malaysia; PHI = Philippines; SIN = Singapore; THA = Thailand; VIE = Viet Nam.

Note: The numbers above (below) each bar refer to the percentage change between 3 March 2025 and 30 May 2025.

Source: *AsianBondsOnline* calculations based on Bloomberg LP data.

Figure I: Chicago Board Options Exchange Volatility Index

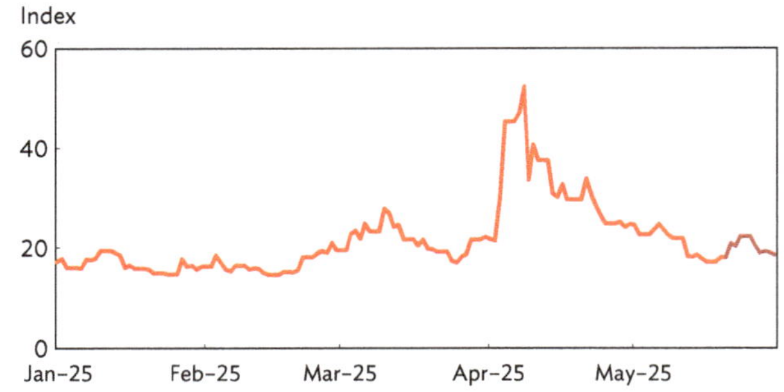

Note: Data are as of 30 May 2025.

Source: Bloomberg LP.

rate environment in the US. In April, US trade policy uncertainty surged to a record high over rising trade tensions between major economies, while US economic policy uncertainty surpassed its previous peak seen during the COVID-19 pandemic (**Figure H**). Financial markets reacted with increased volatility in March–April as investors struggled with the implications of shifting trade dynamics (**Figure I**), before volatility eased in May with the expected progress of trade negotiation between US and its trade partners, especially after the announcement of a trade deal between the PRC and the US. However, any further uncertainty in trade policies could erode investment sentiment and weigh down financial conditions, curtailing investments globally and regionally. Such uncertainty may prolong elevated borrowing costs, heighten market volatility, intensify supply chain disruptions, and slow economic growth. Uncertain trade policies can also raise concerns that the global economy is becoming more divided, thus harming international cooperation, disrupting cross-border capital flows, and weakening the global financial safety net. These developments could significantly heighten systemic financial vulnerabilities and reduce the resilience of the global financial system.

Figure H: United States Policy Uncertainty Indexes

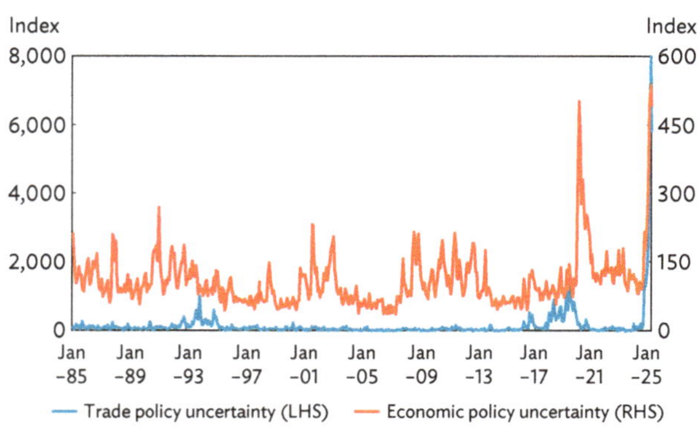

LHS = left-hand side, RHS = right-hand side.

Note: Data are as of May 2025.

Source: https://www.policyuncertainty.com/trade_uncertainty.html (accessed 31 May 2025).

Compounding these risks is the higher-for-longer interest rate environment in the US. The Fed's concern about persistent inflation, driven by the impacts of higher tariffs combined with a resilient economic performance and domestic job market, may prolong the easing cycle. After the May FOMC meeting, the expected likelihood of a 25 bps rate cut in June fell to 3.8% on 30 May from 34.0% on 2 May, and the probability of a 25 bps rate cut in July fell from 55.2% to 24.8%. Meanwhile, the chances of there being no rate cut in June and July rose to 96.2% and 74.3%, respectively, on 30 May from 65.1% and 20.7% on 2 May. The prospect of a higher-for-longer interest rate environment in the US might delay the easing of monetary stances in emerging East Asia as regional central banks maintain current policies to support their domestic currencies, keeping global borrowing costs elevated. Borrowers with high levels of USD-denominated debt and weak fundamentals could face prolonged pressure as persistently high interest rates increase the burden of debt servicing. **Box 1** discusses the challenges that central banks face implementing monetary policy in a high-debt environment.

Other possible downside risks include the potential of wider conflict in the Middle East, which could disrupt supply chains, driving up food and energy prices and increasing global uncertainty. Within the region, further deterioration in the PRC's property sector could potentially exacerbate negative spillovers to household wealth and income prospects, weakening consumer and business sentiment and overall economic activity. This could also lead to lower-than-expected fiscal revenues for local governments and distressed financial positions among property developers and related businesses. In the medium term, extreme weather events could negatively impact growth and inflation.

Box 1: Why High Debt Makes It Harder for Central Banks to Do Their Job

Fueled by low interest rates, expansionary fiscal policies, and accomodative monetary measures to sustain growth and financial stability, public and private debt have grown significantly worldwide since the global financial crisis. While borrowing has supported economic growth, it also raises an important concern: When economies carry a lot of debt, it can make it harder for central banks to do their job—especially when it comes to controlling inflation and keeping the economy stable.

Central banks rely on tools like interest rate changes to influence the economy. For example, if inflation is too high, raising interest rates can help cool things down. But when an economy is carrying a heavy debt load, these tools may not work well. There are several reasons: First, a government may prefer low interest rates to keep borrowing costs down, especially when it has large debts to repay. This can lead to pressure on the central bank to keep rates low, even when inflation is rising. Second, too much public spending can "crowd out" private sector investment, making it more expensive for businesses to borrow and invest—limiting the overall impact of low interest rates. Third, households and firms that are already under a high debt burden may choose to pay down their loans when interest rates are reduced—so the usual boost to the economy is muted. Finally, confidence and debt concerns may make it harder for central banks to keep inflation stable if people and investors start to worry that an economy cannot manage its debt, since they may expect higher inflation in the future and therefore demand higher interest rates.

Qureshi, Jalles, and Tian (forthcoming) look at how well monetary policy—mainly interest rate changes—works in 40 economies, including several in Asia. The paper focuses on how different levels of debt and government spending affect the ability of central banks to influence inflation and economic growth.

To examine these dynamics, a local projection method is employed, which allows for the flexible estimation of impulse response functions without imposing strong assumptions about the data-generating process (Jordà 2005). A smooth transition autoregressive structure is embedded into the local projection framework to capture nonlinear and asymmetric effects of monetary policy across different fiscal regimes (Granger and Teräsvirta 1993). This approach allows monetary transmission to evolve gradually with changing debt levels or fiscal conditions, rather than shifting abruptly at an arbitrary threshold. It also accommodates heterogeneity in institutional frameworks and macro-fiscal structures across economies, making it well-suited to a diverse data sample. The paper identifies a new set of monetary policy shocks for about 40 advanced and emerging economies using the high-frequency forecast error approach based on the methodology of Furceri et al. (2018), which isolates unexpected changes in policy rates from anticipated central bank actions. These shocks are aggregated to an annual frequency to align with macro-fiscal data and estimate dynamic policy effects.

The key findings of Qureshi, Jalles, and Tian (forthcoming) suggest that when debt levels are high, monetary policy becomes less effective (**Figure B1**). When central banks raise interest rates, we typically expect inflation to fall and economic growth to slow. But in economies with high levels of public and private debt, these effects are much weaker. The paper finds output responses to be 30%–50% smaller, and the impact of monetary policy on inflation often disappears completely in high-debt situations. The paper also finds that private debt plays a bigger role in weakening the effects on economic growth, while public debt more directly limits the central bank's ability to lower inflation. The situation gets even more complicated when governments are still spending heavily—that is, when the fiscal stance is expansionary. Under such a scenario, central banks' policies are even less likely to

This box was written by Irfan Qureshi (public sector specialist) and Shu Tian (principal economist) of the Asian Development Bank, and João Tovar Jalles (senior associate professor of economics) at the Lisbon School of Economics and Management, University of Lisbon.

continued on next page

Box 1 *continued*

Figure B1: Conditional Effects of Monetary Policy Shocks on Growth—Private and Public Debt in Emerging Markets and Developing Economies

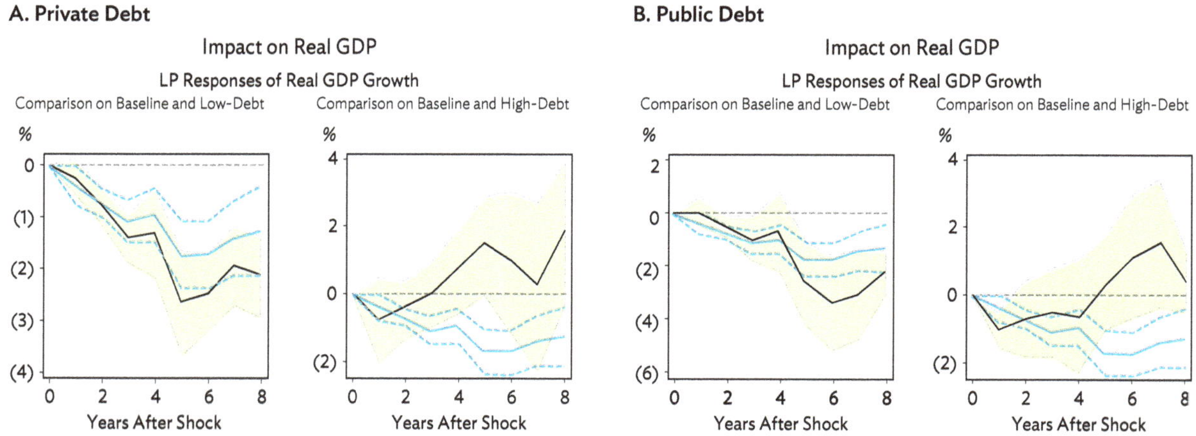

( ) = negative, GDP = gross domestic product, LP = local projection.

Notes: Monetary policy shocks are based on the high-frequency forecast error approach (Furceri et al. 2018) and applied to Consensus Economics data. Point estimates are normalized by one standard deviation of the shock. The solid black lines in the figure plot the impulse responses of shocks on the dependent variable amid the private and public debt regime indicated above each panel. Year = 1 is the first year after a shock took place at year = 0. For example, the position of the line at year = 8 shows the change in real GDP 8 years after the shock. The solid blue line and corresponding dashed blue lines correspond to the baseline unconditional result for better comparison. The green shaded areas display the 90% spatial-correlation-consistent error bands.

Source: Authors' calculations based on data from CEIC Data Company.

work as intended. Interestingly, economies with stronger institutions—especially independent central banks—tend to manage better. These economies see a stronger response to monetary policy, even in high-debt environments. However, simply having rules about government spending (e.g., fiscal rules) does not help much unless those rules are actually implemented.

The policy implications of the study are clear. First, debt must remain sustainable. Managing debt responsibly helps protect both government finances and the effectiveness of central banks. Aims during economic booms should be to reduce deficits and avoid spending spikes. Central bank independence should also be sustained. Central banks must be free to act in the best interest of the economy—especially when it comes to keeping inflation in check—because political or fiscal interference weakens their ability to effectively conduct monetary policy. In addition, since private debt can also dampen monetary policy effectiveness, governments should use macroprudential tools such as regulations on lending and frequent stress testing to limit risky borrowing and protect financial stability. Finally, fiscal and monetary policies should work in the same direction and coordinate as much as possible. For example, governments should keep spending in check when central banks are trying to cool down the economy.

As economies across Asia and the Pacific and other regions try to rebuild after the COVID-19 pandemic, they face a tricky environment: rising inflation, greater policy uncertainty, a slowing global growth outlook, less room to spend, and tighter global financing conditions. In this context, the ability of central banks to act effectively becomes even more critical. Aligning responsible government spending with strong, independent central banks helps to maintain stability, control inflation, and respond to future economic shocks.

References

Furceri, D., P. Loungani, J. Ostry, and P. Pizzuto. 2018. The Effects of Monetary Policy Shocks on Inequality. *Journal of International Money and Finance* 85. pp. 168–186.

Granger, C.W.J., and T. Teräsvirta. 1993. *Modelling Nonlinear Economic Relationships*. Oxford: Oxford University Press.

Jordà, Ò. 2005. Estimation and Inference of Impulse Responses by Local Projections. *American Economic Review* 95 (1). pp. 161–182.

Qureshi, I., J. Jalles, and S. Tian. Forthcoming. Does Monetary Policy Lose Its Bite? The Nonlinear Role of Debt and Fiscal Conditions.

Bond Market Developments in the First Quarter of 2025

Section 1. Local Currency Bonds Outstanding

Growth in the emerging East Asian local currency (LCY) bond market slowed in the first quarter (Q1) of 2025 amid heightened global trade uncertainties.[4] The LCY bond market in emerging East Asia reached a size of USD27.2 trillion at the end of March on moderated growth of 2.7% quarter-on-quarter (q-o-q), compared with 3.1% q-o-q in the previous quarter, amid uncertainties associated with trade policies and negotiations (**Figure 1A**). Both government and corporate bonds experienced slower growth in Q1 2025. The region's LCY government bonds outstanding reached

Figure 1: Local Currency Bonds Outstanding and Issuance

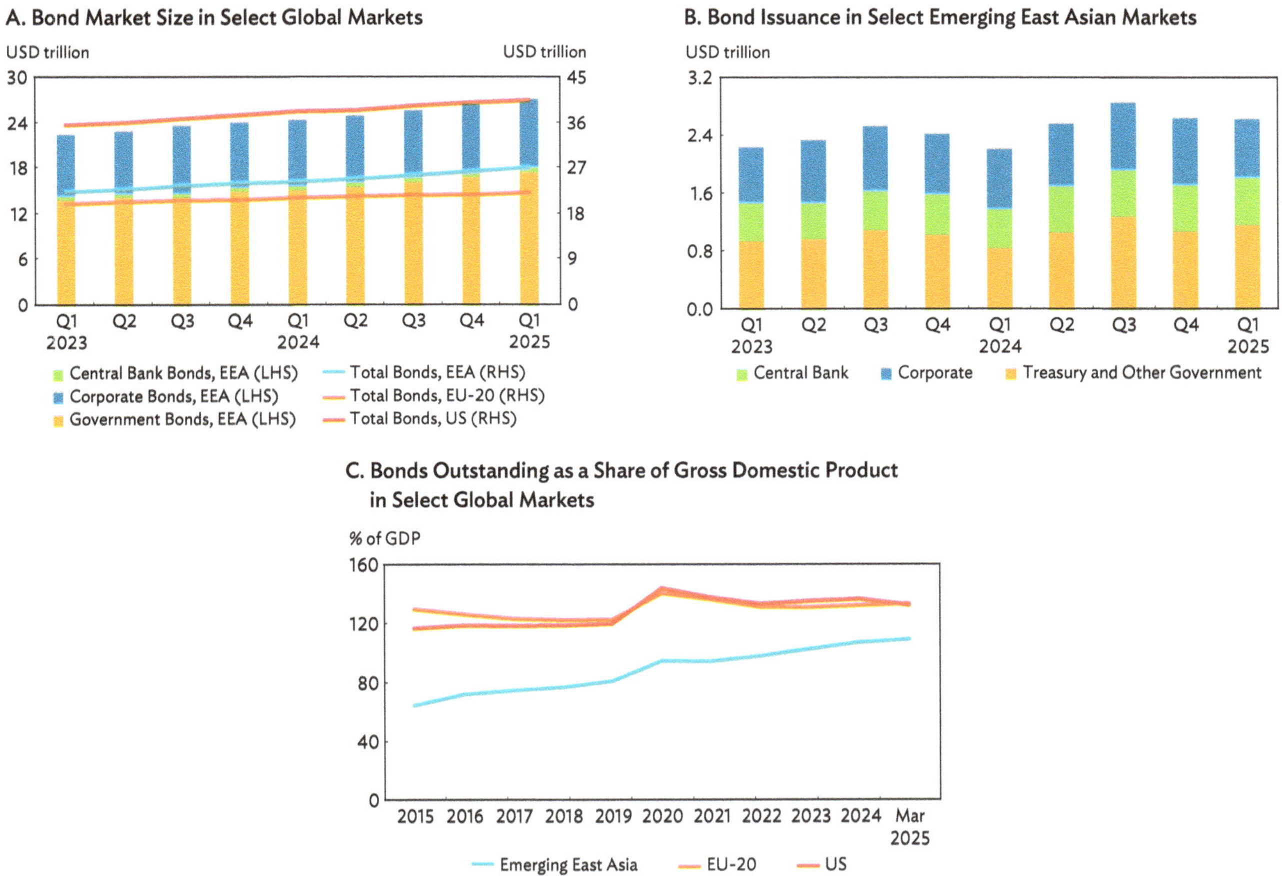

EEA = Emerging East Asia, EU- 20 = European Union 20, GDP = gross domestic product, LHS = left-hand side, RHS = right-hand side, Q1 = first quarter, Q2 = second quarter, Q3 = third quarter, Q4 = fourth quarter, US = United States, USD = United States dollar.

Notes:
1. Emerging East Asia is defined to include the Association of Southeast Asian Nations plus the People's Republic of China; Hong Kong, China; and the Republic of Korea.
2. The EU-20 includes the member markets of Austria, Belgium, Croatia, Cyprus, Estonia, Finland, France, Germany, Greece, Ireland, Italy, Latvia, Lithuania, Luxembourg, Malta, the Netherlands, Portugal, Slovakia, Slovenia, and Spain.

Source: *AsianBondsOnline* calculations based on various local market sources.

[4] Emerging East Asia is defined to include member states of the Association of Southeast Asian Nations plus the People's Republic of China; Hong Kong, China; and the Republic of Korea.

USD17.5 trillion at the end of March on moderated growth of 3.8% q-o-q, compared with 4.0% q-o-q in the previous quarter, as a large volume of maturities in the People's Republic of China (PRC) capped regional growth in Q1 2025. Meanwhile, expansion in the region's LCY corporate bond stock eased to 1.0% q-o-q in Q1 2025 from 1.6% q-o-q in the prior quarter as corporate bond issuance contracted over uncertainty in global trade policies and the growth outlook (**Figure 1B**). At the end of March, the emerging East Asian bond market's size relative to gross domestic product (GDP) reached 109.9%, compared with 134.6% in the European Union 20 (EU-20) and 133.5% in the United States (US) (**Figure 1C**). Despite the uncertainties, outstanding LCY bonds in emerging East Asia expanded faster than in the EU-20 (1.7% q-o-q) and the US (1.4% q-o-q), partly driven by regional governments front-loading their borrowing. **Box 2** discusses how capital market development has helped firms efficiently deploy capital and become more productive, especially in low- and middle-income economies.

Box 2: Capital Market Financing in Low- and Middle-Income Economies

Over the past 3 decades, capital market financing has surged for firms in low- and middle-income economies. This growth is not confined to a few established corporations but includes a broad spectrum of firms from an increasing number of economies.[a] Firms are deploying this capital to become more productive—investing in physical assets, hiring more workers, and expanding operations—spurring growth both at the firm level and within their domestic economies.

Firms from low- and middle-income economies raised cumulative net capital issuance (CNI) of USD4.0 trillion from bond and equity markets between 1990 and 2022 (**Figure B2.1**). From 2000 to 2022, CNI increased fourfold in middle-income economies and eightfold in low-income economies. Over the same period, CNI in these two groups of economies doubled as a share of gross domestic product (GDP) while also growing faster than bank financing.

Figure B2.1: Firms' Cumulative Capital Market Financing in Low- and Middle-Income Economies—Globally and in East Asia and the Pacific

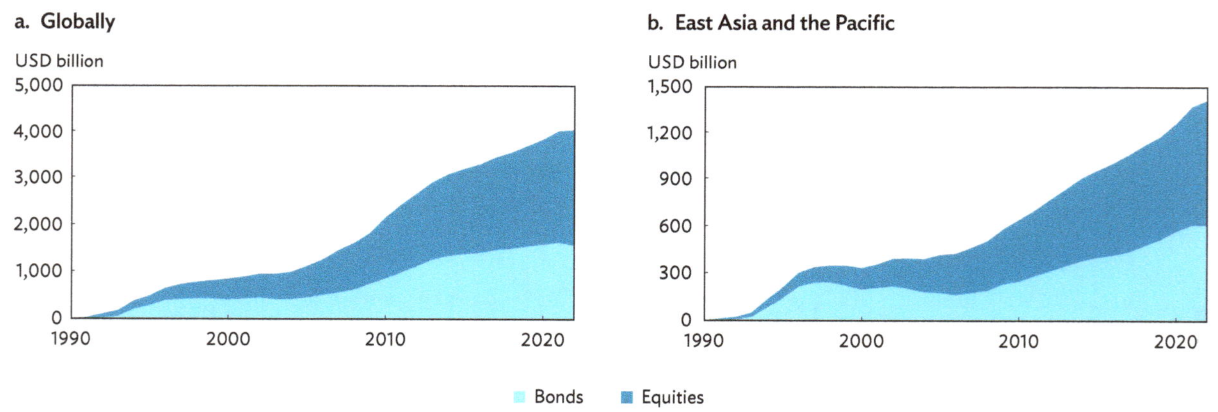

USD = United States dollar.

Note: USD values are in constant 2020 dollars. Cumulative net capital issuance is calculated for each year as the sum of equity and bond issuances since 1990 minus the value of bonds that have matured since 1990.

Source: Authors' calculations based on issuance data from LSEG's Securities Data Company Platinum database.

This box was written by Cesaire Meh (manager, Macro and Market Risk, Economic and Market Research Department) at the International Finance Corporation and Sergio Schmukler (research manager, Macroeconomics and Growth, Development Economics) at the World Bank, jointly with Matias Soria (research assistant) at the International Finance Corporation and World Bank. This box is a brief summary of a report by C. A. Meh and S. L. Schmukler, eds. 2025. *Financing Firm Growth: The Role of Capital Markets in Low- and Middle-Income Countries.* Washington, DC: World Bank. Graphs from the report for different economies and regions are available in the accompanying Capital Markets Portal. This box relies on the World Bank's economy income classification. Low- and middle-income economies are broken down into two subgroups: (i) middle-income; and (ii) low-income, excluding the People's Republic of China. The People's Republic of China is treated separately due to its economic ascent and size, which could otherwise distort the analysis for other economies in the same category. Economies are assigned into income groups based upon their World Bank income classification as of 1990.

[a] The analysis focuses on nonfinancial firms participating in capital markets during 1990–2022. Although these firms are a small fraction of the total number of firms, they typically account for a large share of national income as they tend to be large firms.

continued on next page

Box 2 *continued*

Domestic bond and equity markets, primarily comprising assets denominated in local currencies, have been the driving force behind this growth. Between 1990 and 2022, domestic markets accounted for more than half of total issuance (53% for bonds and 79% for equities). Moreover, the average size of individual domestic bond issuances for firms raising funds in capital markets for the first time decreased by about 30% from 2000–2009 to 2010–2022. Since small firms typically issue smaller amounts, the decline in the average size of domestic bond issuance suggests that accessing domestic capital markets became easier for them.

A similar pattern is observed for firms in low- and middle-income economies within East Asia and the Pacific, where CNI reached USD1.4 trillion in 2022 (**Figure B2.1b**). During the entire review period, this region exhibited the largest CNI-to-GDP ratio, reaching a value of 30% in 2022, compared with an average CNI-to-GDP ratio of 23% observed across all other low- and middle-income economies globally. The relevance of domestic markets as a driving force was particularly important within East Asia and the Pacific, as the average share of domestic CNI was 83% during 2010–2022, compared with 71% for all other low- and middle-income economies.

As capital markets expanded, a broader range of firms gained access to financing, with a greater share of funds allocated to smaller, younger, more productive, and financially more constrained firms than those already participating in capital markets. In particular, 14,000 firms started issuing only after the year 2000, while only around 1,800 publicly listed firms were active before then. These new participants in capital markets accounted for more than 60% of CNI in low- and middle-income economies by 2022. Moreover, firms from 32 middle-income economies and 13 low-income economies accessed capital markets for the first time during this period.

At the time of issuance, new participants in low- and middle-income economies had higher marginal returns to capital (defined as the additional output a company generates from using an extra unit of capital) than firms in the same industry and economy that were active in capital markets in the 1990s. For this reason, investing in these firms had the potential to yield greater profits and increase production, making them particularly effective recipients of new capital.

The impact of capital market participation on firms and the broader economy hinges on whether firms use the funds raised for productive activities. Effectively, in the first year after raising capital, firms' investment in physical capital—measured as firms' property, plant, and equipment—rose 16% in low-income economies and 8% in middle-income economies, with some of these effects persisting for years (**Figure B2.2**). East Asia and the Pacific experienced the largest real effect from capital market financing across all regions, with a 16% increase in physical capital. In all cases, this growth was associated with an increase in both employment and sales.

Figure B2.2: Growth in Firms' Physical Capital in Low- and Middle-Income Economies After Capital Market Issuance

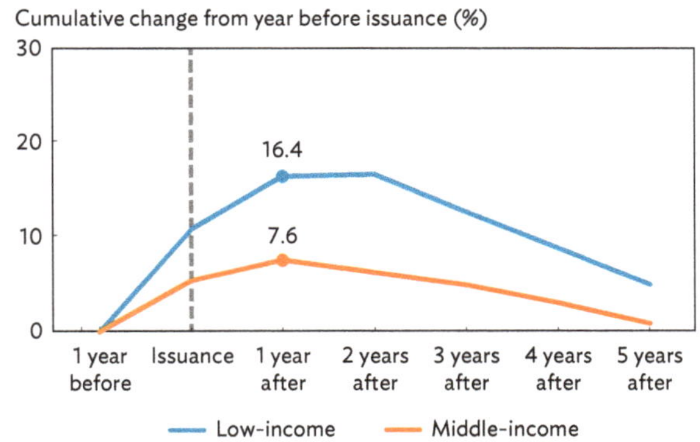

Note: The baseline for estimating cumulative impact is the year before issuance.

Sources: Authors' calculations based on issuance data from LSEG's Securities Data Company Platinum database and Worldscope balance sheet data.

The effects of capital market issuances on firm growth vary depending on the issuer and the financial instrument used. The impact on growth is particularly strong for new participants despite their smaller issuances, as it appears to alleviate their financial constraints. The positive effects on firm growth are twice as strong for equity issuances as for all bond issuances (including refinancing)—perhaps reflecting the greater flexibility that equity financing provides without the pressure of regular, fixed debt payments.

At the economy-wide level, the findings suggest that capital is being allocated more efficiently. Firms' participation in capital markets is linked to increases in an economy's total stock of physical capital and employment levels. In low-income economies, firm issuance activity accounted for 21% of the growth in physical capital and 12% of the growth in employment among publicly listed firms between 2000 and 2022. In middle-income economies, these estimates were 22% and 20%, respectively. Because firms with higher marginal returns to capital raised more funds, markets allocated capital more efficiently across firms, resulting in a greater impact on output. New participants in capital markets in the 2000s were especially important drivers of these positive effects.

Expansion in the PRC bond market led the region's LCY bond market growth in Q1 2025 (Figure 2A). The PRC's bond market expanded 3.0% q-o-q as the government tapped the bond market to finance stimulus measures and support the economy. The PRC, along with Hong Kong, China, drove the expansion of the region's LCY bond market as a share of GDP (**Figure 2B**). The Republic of Korea's outstanding LCY bond stock rose to USD2.3 trillion, on growth of 0.8% q-o-q in Q1 2025, and accounted for 8.3% of the regional bond stock at the end of March. The aggregate LCY bond stock among members of the Association of Southeast Asian Nations (ASEAN) reached USD2.5 trillion at the end of March, comprising 9.1% of the regional total, on growth of 2.2% q-o-q. Outstanding Treasury bonds in emerging East Asia totaled USD17.5 trillion at the end of March, accounting for 64.4% of the region's LCY bond market, while corporate bonds (USD9.0 trillion) and central bank bonds (USD0.7 trillion) represented the remaining 33.2% and 2.4%, respectively (**Figure 2C**). At the end of March, 55.6% of outstanding Treasury bonds in the region had a remaining tenor of over 5 years (**Figure 2D**). The size-weighted average tenor of Treasury bonds outstanding in emerging East Asia was 8.4 years at the end of March, slightly longer than that of the US (7.8 years) but broadly comparable to that of the EU-20 (8.3 years).

Figure 2: Local Currency Bonds Outstanding in Select Emerging East Asian Markets

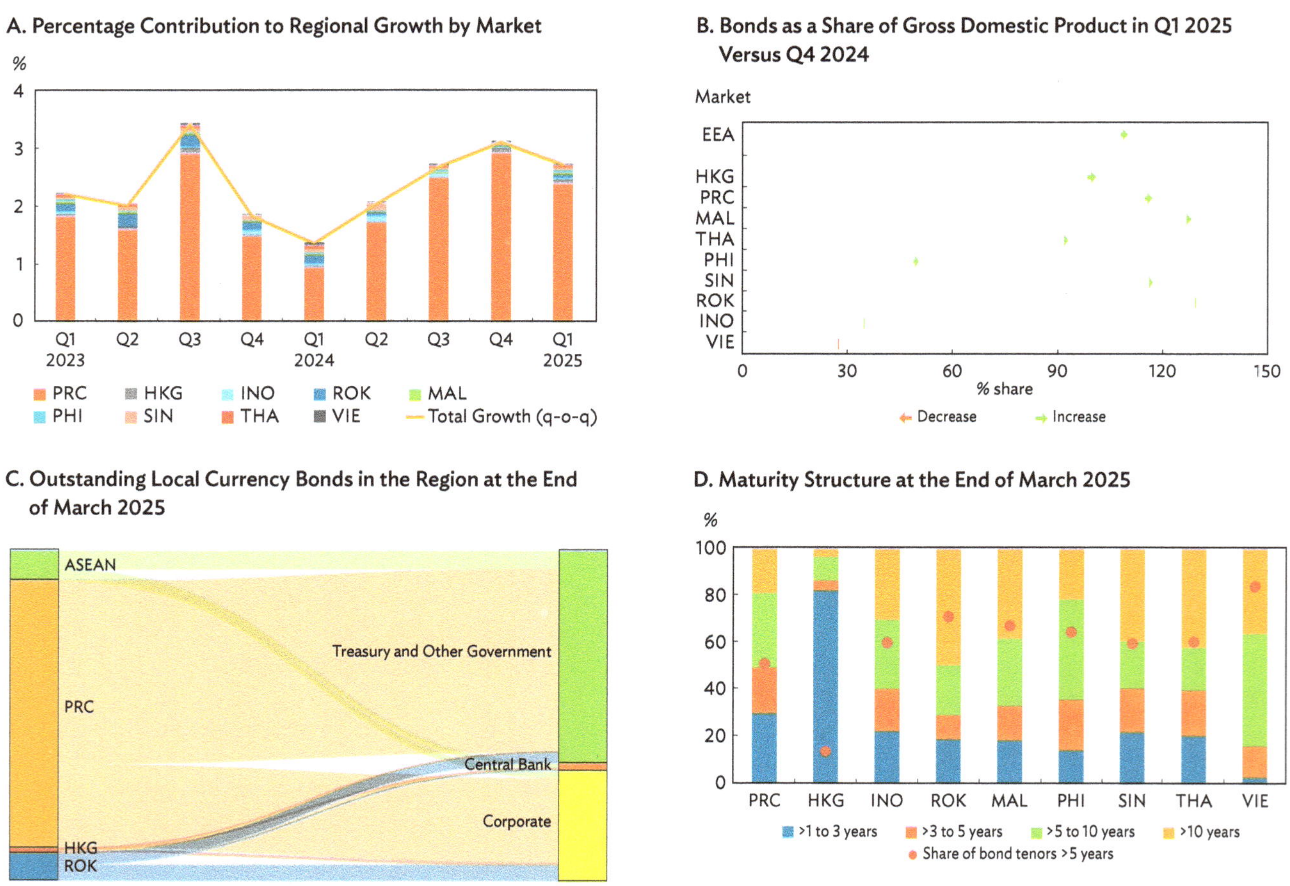

ASEAN = Association of Southeast Asian Nations; PRC = People's Republic of China; EEA = emerging East Asia; HKG = Hong Kong, China; INO = Indonesia; ROK = Republic of Korea; MAL = Malaysia; PHI = Philippines; Q1 = first quarter; Q4 = fourth quarter; q-o-q = quarter-on-quarter; SIN = Singapore; THA = Thailand; VIE = Viet Nam.

Notes:

1. Emerging East Asia is defined to include the Association of Southeast Asian Nations plus the People's Republic of China; Hong Kong, China; and the Republic of Korea.
2. Growth rates are calculated from a local currency base and do not include currency effects. For emerging East Asia, growth figures are based on 31 March 2025 currency exchange rates and do not include currency effects.
3. GDP data are from CEIC Data Company.

Source: *AsianBondsOnline* calculations based on various local market sources.

Banks remained a significant holder of LCY Treasury bonds at the end of March, while investor diversification in the region's bond markets continued to improve in Q1 2025. Banks held approximately 34.8% of emerging East Asian LCY Treasury bonds at the end of March, followed by insurance and pension funds (29.2%) (**Figure 3**). Banks' holding share was down from 36.7% in the same period a year earlier as nearly all markets posted declines in their respective bank holding shares. Meanwhile, other investor groups saw upticks in their respective investor holdings shares. The share of Treasury bonds held by insurance and pension funds slightly rose from 28.8% to 29.2% between Q1 2024 and Q1 2025. Moreover, central bank holdings in the region rose the most to 5.9% at the end of March from 5.1% a year earlier, largely due to an increase in the Treasury bond holdings of Bank Indonesia from 21.3% to 26.4% as the central bank ramped up its holdings in support of monetary operations. In terms of market concentration, as measured by the Herfindahl–Hirschman Index, the region's LCY Treasury bond markets continued to see declining scores, demonstrating more diverse investor profiles.[5] On the other hand, index scores in the PRC and Viet Nam remained high as LCY Treasury bond holdings were concentrated among a few types of investors in these two markets.

Figure 3: Investor Profiles of Local Currency Treasury Bonds in Select Emerging East Asian Markets

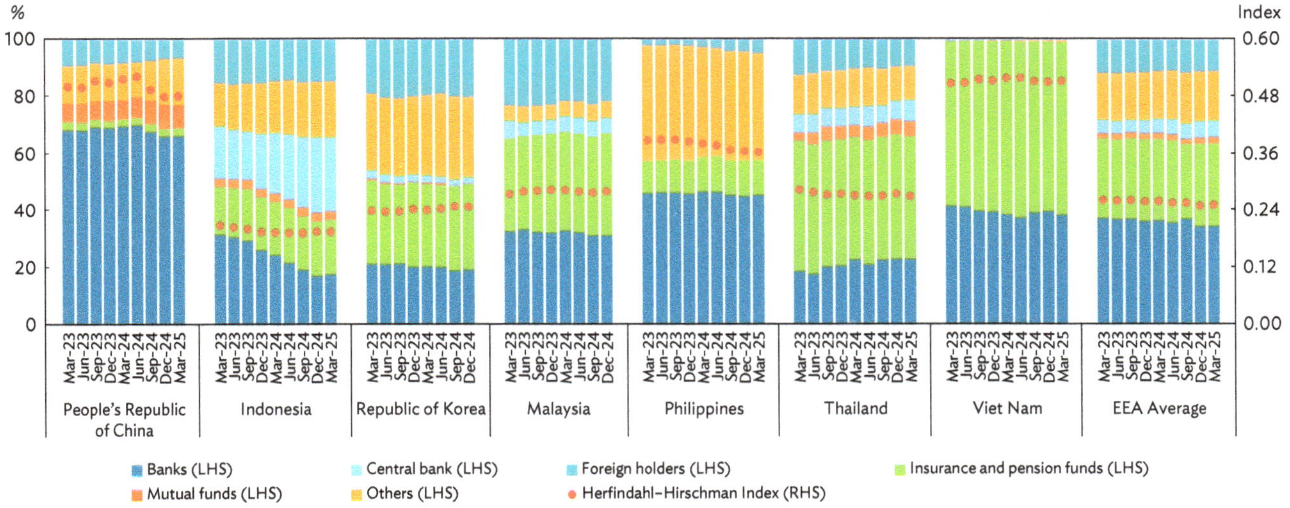

EEA = emerging East Asia, LHS = left-hand side, RHS = right-hand side.

Notes:

1. Data for the Republic of Korea and the Malaysia are up to December 2024.
2. "Others" include government institutions, individuals, securities companies, custodians, private corporations, and all other investors not elsewhere classified.
3. The Herfindahl-Hirschman Index is a commonly accepted measure of market concentration. In this case, the index was used to measure the investor profile diversification of the local currency bond markets and is calculated by summing the squared share of each investor group in the bond market.

Sources: People's Republic of China (CEIC Data Company); Indonesia (Directorate General of Budget Financing and Risk Management, Ministry of Finance); Republic of Korea (Bank of Korea); Malaysia (Bank Negara Malaysia); Philippines (Bureau of the Treasury); Thailand (Bank of Thailand); and Viet Nam (Ministry of Finance).

[5] The Herfindahl–Hirschman Index is a commonly accepted measure of market concentration. The index is used to measure the investor profile diversification of the region's local currency bond markets and is calculated by summing the squared share of each investor group in the bond market.

Section 2. Local Currency Bond Issuance

LCY bond issuance in emerging East Asia marginally contracted in Q1 2025 due to reduced corporate bond financing amid economic uncertainty. Total LCY bond issuance inched down 0.5% q-o-q in Q1 2025 to USD2.6 trillion as the contraction in the corporate bond market more than offset growth in the government bond segment (**Figure 4A**). Issuance of government bonds rose 8.1% q-o-q in Q1 2025 as nearly all markets in the region registered higher quarterly issuance volumes. The PRC, which accounted for 86.7% of total regional government bond issuance in Q1 2025, led the growth as the government ramped up issuance to support the economy (**Figure 4B**). In addition, issuance of government bonds in the Republic of Korea and ASEAN markets surged 79.5% q-o-q and 17.4% q-o-q, respectively, in line with their front-loading policies at the start of the year. Meanwhile, total corporate bond sales in Q1 2025 contracted 12.1% q-o-q, with seven out of nine regional markets posting contractions. This was partly due to reduced financing demands by companies amid economic uncertainty and weakened investor appetite brought about by ongoing global trade tensions.

Figure 4: Local Currency Bond Issuance in Select Emerging East Asian Markets

A. Percentage Contribution to Regional Growth by Bond Type

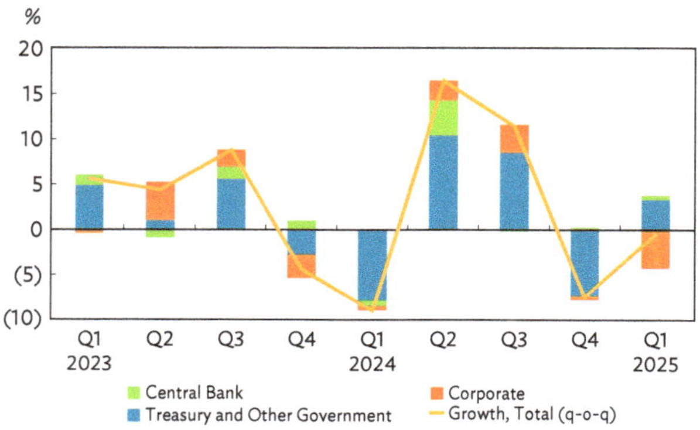

B. Local Currency Bond Issuance in the First Quarter of 2025

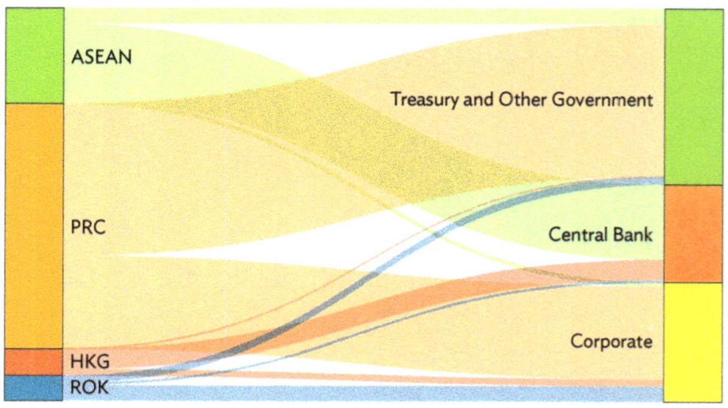

( ) = negative; ASEAN = Association of Southeast Asian Nations; PRC = People's Republic of China; HKG = Hong Kong, China; ROK = Republic of Korea; Q1 = first quarter; Q2 = second quarter; Q3 = third quarter; Q4 = fourth quarter; q-o-q = quarter-on-quarter.

Notes:

1. ASEAN comprises the markets of Indonesia, Malaysia, the Philippines, Singapore, Thailand, and Viet Nam.
2. Figures were computed based on 31 March 2025 currency exchange rates and do not include currency effects.

Source: *AsianBondsOnline* calculations based on various local market sources.

LCY government bond issuance in emerging East Asia continued to mainly comprise medium- to long-term maturities, but the share of short-term bonds increased in Q1 2025. The share of government bonds issued with maturities of more than 5 years declined to 51.2% during the quarter from 55.3% in the fourth quarter (Q4) of 2024 (**Figure 5A**). Thus, the size-weighted average maturity of Treasury bond issuance in emerging East Asia declined to 7.0 years in Q1 2025 from 8.0 years in the previous quarter (**Figure 6A**). The decline was largely driven by the PRC, where the share of bonds issued with maturities of more than 5 years fell from 54.4% in Q4 2024 to 38.6% in Q1 2025 (**Figure 5B**), as the market had previously issued a large amount of long-term LCY bonds in Q4 2024. In Hong Kong, China, however, the share of LCY government bond issuance with maturities of more than 5 years rose to 33.3% in Q1 2025 from 0.6% in the previous quarter as the government issued longer-term bonds as part of its issuance schedule. The size-weighted average maturities in the PRC and Hong Kong, China were both below 6 years, while the Republic of Korea had the longest average maturity of 14.5 years (**Figure 6B**). Meanwhile, the average maturity in ASEAN markets fell to 9.1 years from 11.5 years in Q4 2024. Issuance in ASEAN markets continued to be largely concentrated in longer maturities of more than 5 years, with Viet Nam (96.2%), the Philippines (93.7%), and Malaysia (82.1%) having the highest percentages of such maturities as a share of total issuance in Q1 2025. Thus, they also had the longest average issuance maturities during the quarter at 11.5 years in Malaysia, 10.2 years in Viet Nam, and 10.0 years in the Philippines.

Figure 5: Maturity Structure of Local Currency Treasury Bond Issuance in Select Emerging East Asian Markets

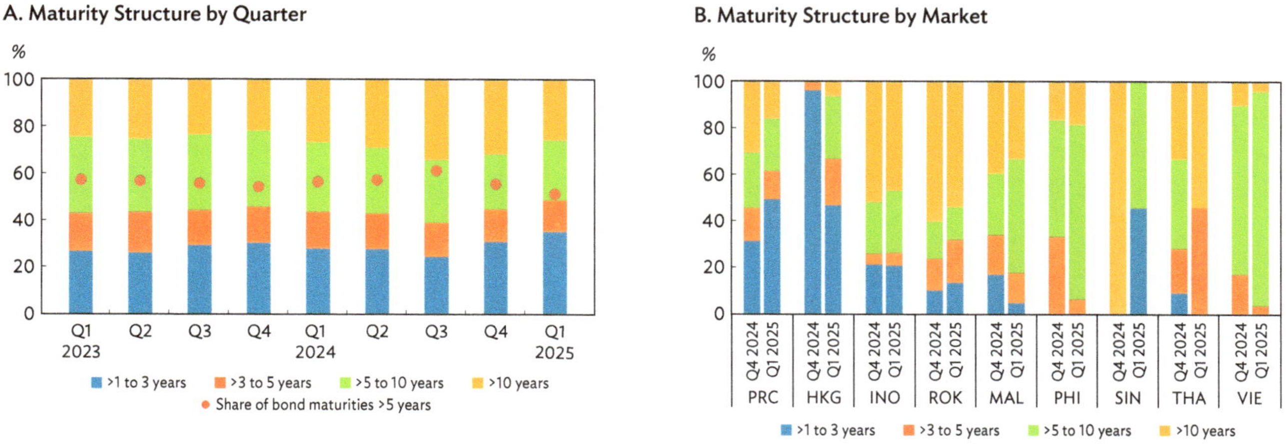

PRC = People's Republic of China; HKG = Hong Kong, China; INO = Indonesia; ROK = Republic of Korea; MAL = Malaysia; PHI = Philippines; Q1 = first quarter; Q2 = second quarter; Q3 = third quarter; Q4 = fourth quarter; SIN = Singapore; THA = Thailand; VIE = Viet Nam.

Notes:

1. Figures were computed based on 31 March 2025 currency exchange rates and do not include currency effects.
2. Treasury bonds are local-currency-denominated, fixed-income securities issued by a government with maturities longer than 1 year.

Source: *AsianBondsOnline* calculations based on various local market sources.

Figure 6: Average Size-Weighted Maturity of Treasury Bond Issuance in Select Emerging East Asian Markets

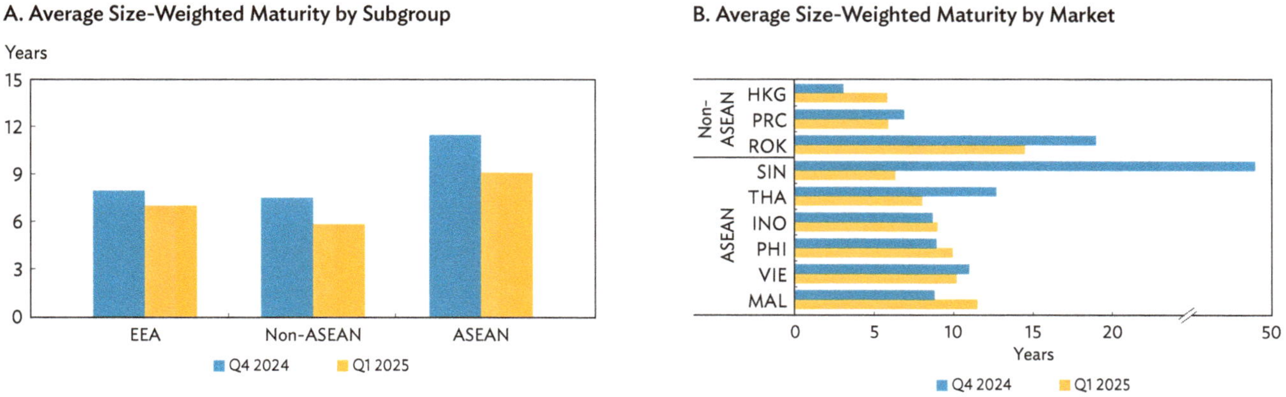

ASEAN = Association of Southeast Asian Nations; PRC = People's Republic of China; EEA = emerging East Asia; HKG = Hong Kong, China; INO = Indonesia; ROK = Republic of Korea; MAL = Malaysia; PHI = Philippines; Q1 = first quarter; Q4 = fourth quarter; SIN = Singapore; THA = Thailand; VIE = Viet Nam.

Notes:

1. Figures were computed based on 31 March 2025 currency exchange rates and do not include currency effects.
2. Treasury bonds are local-currency-denominated, fixed-income securities issued by a government with maturities longer than 1 year.

Source: *AsianBondsOnline* calculations based on various local market sources.

Section 3: Intra-Regional Bond Issuance

Heightened global economic uncertainties weighed on intra-regional bond issuance in emerging East Asia in Q1 2025.[6] The region's intra-regional bond issuance tallied USD7.7 billion in Q1 2025, down 31.0% q-o-q from the previous quarter's USD11.2 billion. The decline was largely driven by decreased debt sales from Hong Kong, China; Malaysia; and Singapore (**Figure 7A**). Meanwhile, the Republic of Korea recorded a 56.5% q-o-q increase in issuance, totaling USD0.8 billion, as corporate issuers sought to diversify their financing sources. During the quarter, PRC-based firms Bocom Leasing and Xtep International Holdings sold a total of USD0.1 billion worth of HKD-denominated bonds, marking the PRC's return to the intra-regional bond market following its last issuance in July 2024. In Q1 2025, Hong Kong, China remained the region's top intra-regional issuer, accounting for 80.8% of the total. By sector, transportation led all others, accounting for 38.1% of the regional total, while the Chinese yuan was the dominant currency of issuance in emerging East Asia during the quarter with an 83.7% share (**Figure 7B**). Among corporate issuers, China Merchants Group—a state-owned logistics firm based in Hong Kong, China—remained the top issuer in the region with aggregate issuance of USD2.5 billion, equivalent to 32.2% of the regional total. This was followed by

Figure 7: Intra-Regional Bond Issuance in Select Emerging East Asian Markets

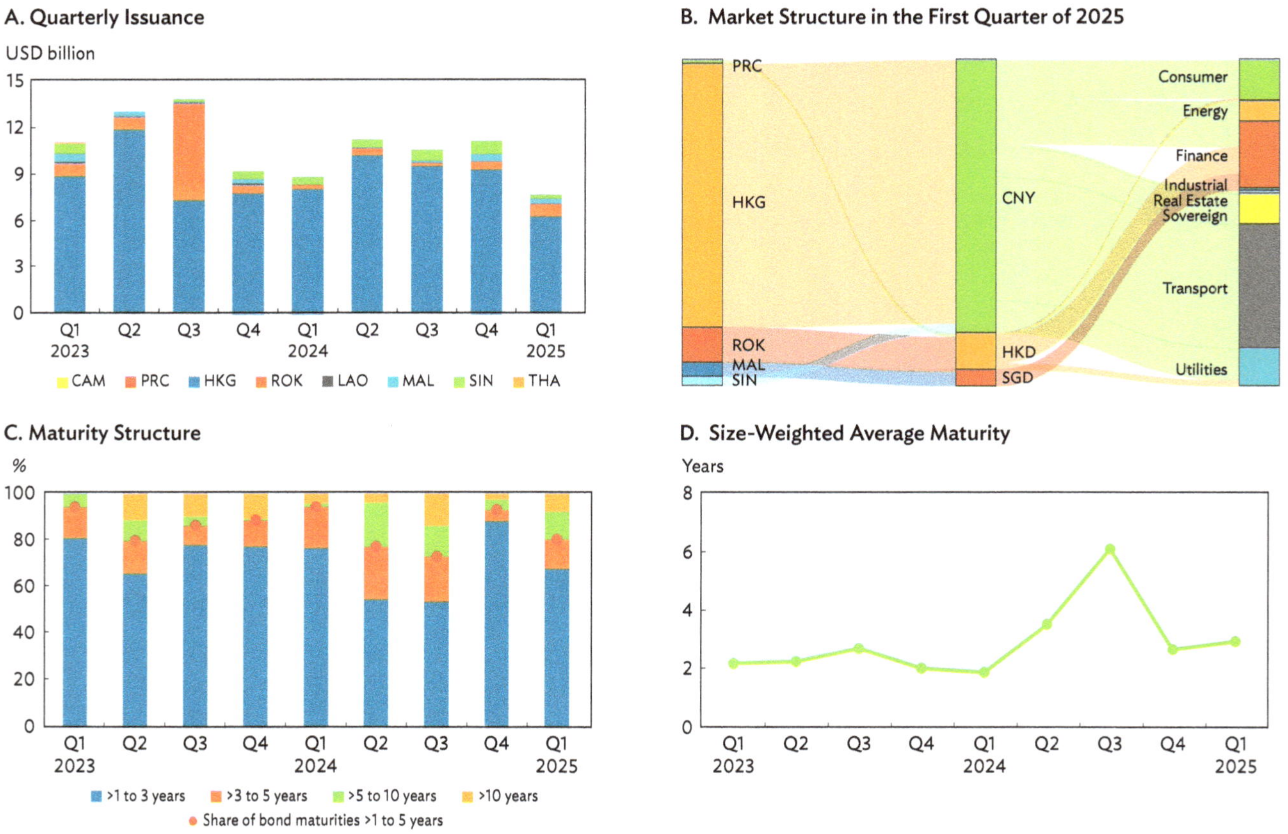

CAM = Cambodia; PRC = People's Republic of China; CNY = Chinese yuan; HKD = Hong Kong dollar; HKG = Hong Kong, China; ROK = Republic of Korea; LAO = Lao People's Democratic Republic; MAL = Malaysia; Q1 = first quarter; Q2 = second quarter; Q3 = third quarter; Q4 = fourth quarter; SGD = Singapore dollar; SIN = Singapore; THA = Thailand; USD = United States dollar.

Notes:

1. Emerging East Asia is defined to include member states of the Association of Southeast Asian Nations plus the People's Republic of China; Hong Kong, China; and the Republic of Korea.
2. Intra-regional bond issuance is defined as emerging East Asian bond issuance denominated in a regional currency excluding the issuer's home currency.
3. Figures were computed based on 31 March 2025 currency exchange rates and do not include currency effects.

Source: *AsianBondsOnline* calculations based on Bloomberg LP data.

[6] Intra-regional bond issuance is defined as emerging East Asian bond issuance denominated in a regional currency excluding the issuer's home currency.

China Tourism Group, a consumer firm also based in Hong Kong, China, with total debt sale of USD0.8 billion, equivalent to 10.7% of the regional total. Intra-regional bond issuances in Q1 2025 included the increased presence of sustainable bonds. Among them were entities from Hong Kong, China, China Water Affairs and China Everbright Greentech, that issued CNY-denominated blue bonds and green bonds, respectively, worth USD137.8 million each. Also, Korea Hydro and Nuclear Power, based in the Republic of Korea, issued HKD-denominated green bonds worth USD149.9 million. About 80.0% of total intra-regional bond issuances in Q1 2025 carried maturities of 5 years or less (**Figure 7C**). This led to a size-weighted average maturity of 3.0 years, up from the previous quarter's 2.7 years (**Figure 7D**).

Section 4. G3 Currency Bond Issuance

Emerging East Asian G3 currency bond issuance rebounded in Q1 2025, particularly in the latter part of the quarter, largely driven by corporates on the broad strengthening of regional currencies against the US dollar.[7] G3 currency bond issuance in the region rose 18.9% q-o-q to USD72.7 billion in Q1 2025, reversing the previous quarter's 14.6% q-o-q contraction, with issuance surging in March to USD33.0 billion (**Figure 8A**). Several regional economies displayed

Figure 8: G3 Currency Bond Issuance in Select Emerging East Asian Markets

A. Monthly Bond Issuance

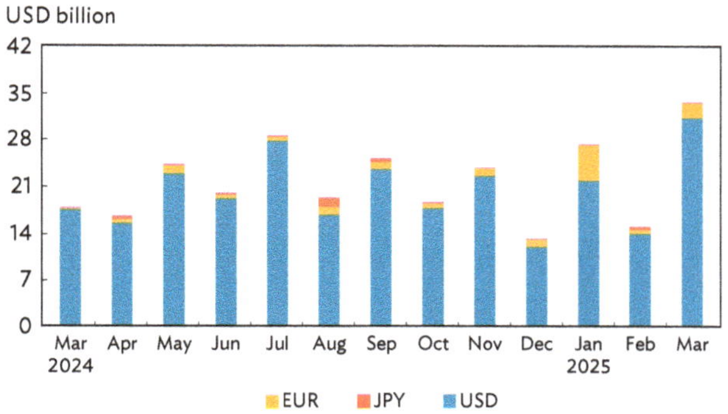

B. Market Share in the First Quarter of 2025

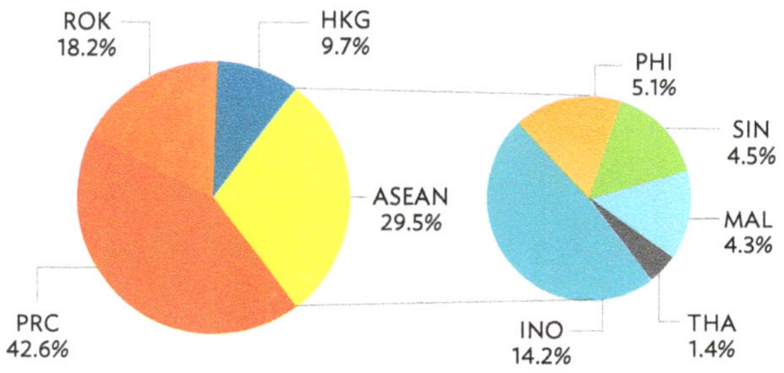

C. Maturity Structure

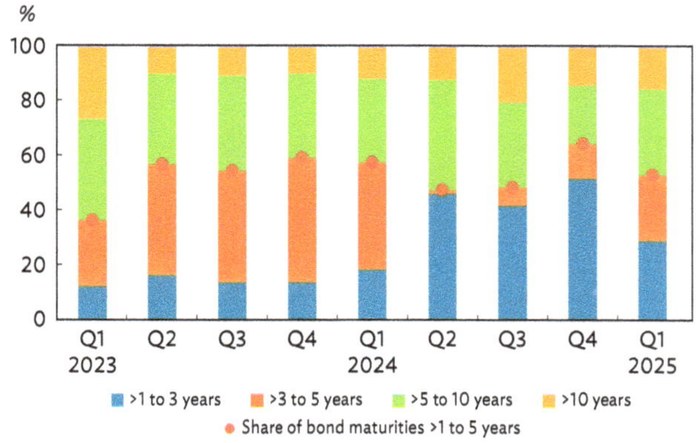

D. Average Size-Weighted Maturity by Subgroup

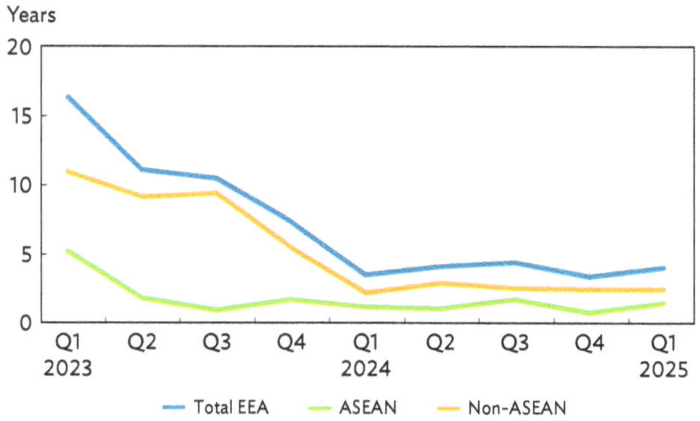

ASEAN = Association of Southeast Asian Nations; PRC = People's Republic of China; EEA = emerging East Asia; EUR = euro; HKG = Hong Kong, China; INO = Indonesia; JPY = Japanese yen; ROK = Republic of Korea; MAL = Malaysia; PHI = Philippines; Q1 = first quarter; Q2 = second quarter; Q3 = third quarter; Q4 = fourth quarter; SIN = Singapore; THA = Thailand; USD = United States dollar.

Notes:

1. ASEAN comprises the markets of Indonesia, Malaysia, the Philippines, Singapore, Thailand, and Viet Nam.
2. Emerging East Asia is defined to include member states of the Association of Southeast Asian Nations plus the People's Republic of China; Hong Kong, China; and the Republic of Korea.
3. G3 currency bonds are denominated in either euros, Japanese yen, or United States dollars.
4. Figures were computed based on 31 March 2025 currency exchange rates and do not include currency effects.

Source: *AsianBondsOnline* calculations based on Bloomberg LP data.

[7] G3 currency bonds are bonds denominated in either euros, Japanese yen, or United States dollars.

significant q-o-q issuance growth, including Hong Kong, China (84.5%); the Republic of Korea (82.8%); and Indonesia (20.2%). Some of the largest issuers were central banks. Bank Indonesia issued USD4.6 billion worth of USD-denominated bonds to support its monetary operations, and Airport Authority Hong Kong issued USD4.2 billion of USD-denominated bonds to fund its capital expenditures and other corporate expenses. ASEAN economies accounted for 29.5% of regional G3 bond issuance in Q1 2025 with USD21.4 billion, reflecting growth of 32.4% q-o-q, as issuance increased in all ASEAN markets except for Singapore (**Figure 8B**). The PRC, which had the region's most issuance during the quarter, witnessed an 8.7% q-o-q decline, partly due to the base effect resulting from USD4.1 billion of government bond issuance in Q4 2024, which was equivalent to 12.0% of the PRC's quarterly total. The top issuer of G3 currency bonds in the region in Q1 2025 was the PRC's state-backed Sino-Ocean Group, issuing USD5.7 billion worth of USD-denominated bonds as part of its debt restructuring plan. About half (53.1%) of G3 bond issuance in Q1 2025 comprised short-term maturities of 5 years or less (**Figure 8C**). The size-weighted average maturity of regional G3 bond issuance rose to 4.1 years in Q1 2025 from 3.4 years in Q4 2024, partly due to declining interest rates (**Figure 8D**).

Appendix

Table A1: Size and Composition of Select Emerging East Asian Local Currency Bond Markets

	Q1 2024		Q4 2024		Q1 2025			Growth Rate (%) Q1 2025	
	Amount (USD billion)	% of GDP	Amount (USD billion)	% of GDP	Amount (USD billion)	% share	% of GDP	q-o-q	y-o-y
People's Republic of China									
Total	19,667	108.7	21,252	115.0	22,012	100.0	117.2	3.0	12.5
Treasury and Other Government	13,031	72.0	14,440	78.1	15,090	68.6	80.3	3.9	16.4
Central Bank	2	0.01	2	0.01	0	0.0	0.0	(100.0)	(100.0)
Corporate	6,634	36.7	6,810	36.8	6,922	31.4	36.9	1.0	4.8
Hong Kong, China									
Total	389	100.5	403	98.5	417	100.0	101.2	3.8	6.6
Treasury and Other Government	37	9.5	39	9.6	40	9.5	9.6	1.8	7.5
Central Bank	162	41.8	168	41.2	169	40.6	41.1	0.9	3.9
Corporate	190	49.1	195	47.8	208	49.9	50.5	6.6	8.7
Indonesia									
Total	428	32.1	477	34.7	473	100.0	34.8	1.9	15.5
Treasury and Other Government	370	27.8	387	28.1	386	81.7	28.4	2.7	8.9
Central Bank	29	2.2	61	4.5	58	12.2	4.2	(3.4)	110.3
Corporate	29	2.2	29	2.1	29	6.1	2.1	2.2	5.0
Republic of Korea									
Total	2,426	133.4	2,241	129.0	2,257	100.0	129.3	0.8	1.7
Treasury and Other Government	906	49.8	847	48.8	869	38.5	49.8	2.6	4.8
Central Bank	89	4.9	79	4.5	75	3.3	1.8	(4.0)	(7.4)
Corporate	1,431	78.7	1,315	75.7	1,313	58.2	75.2	(0.1)	0.3
Malaysia									
Total	432	128.7	468	126.8	482	100.0	128.4	2.3	4.9
Treasury and Other Government	250	74.3	273	73.9	282	58.4	74.9	2.4	6.0
Central Bank	3	0.8	0	0.0	0	0.0	0.0	–	(100.0)
Corporate	180	53.5	195	52.9	201	41.6	53.4	2.0	5.0
Philippines									
Total	219	49.5	223	48.9	235	100.0	50.0	4.1	9.4
Treasury and Other Government	180	40.9	187	40.8	196	83.5	41.7	4.1	10.8
Central Bank	14	3.1	14	3.0	16	6.7	3.4	15.3	18.0
Corporate	25	5.6	23	5.1	23	9.8	4.9	(2.8)	(5.1)
Singapore									
Total	577	112.9	622	116.1	646	100.0	117.0	2.0	11.3
Treasury and Other Government	208	40.7	225	42.0	237	36.7	43.0	3.5	13.3
Central Bank	228	44.6	249	46.5	257	39.9	46.6	1.5	12.2
Corporate	141	27.6	148	27.6	151	23.4	27.4	0.7	6.9
Thailand									
Total	465	93.8	501	91.9	512	100.0	92.9	1.8	2.6
Treasury and Other Government	269	54.2	297	54.4	306	59.7	55.5	2.6	6.1
Central Bank	65	13.1	69	12.6	73	14.2	13.2	6.0	5.0
Corporate	132	26.6	136	24.9	133	26.1	24.2	(2.0)	(5.7)
Viet Nam									
Total	116	27.4	124	27.5	126	100.0	27.4	1.9	11.6
Treasury and Other Government	81	19.0	87	19.3	91	71.9	19.7	4.4	15.8
Central Bank	7	1.6	5	1.2	4	2.9	0.8	(32.1)	(45.4)
Corporate	29	6.8	32	7.0	32	25.2	6.9	1.0	13.7
Emerging East Asia									
Total	24,721	103.7	26,311	108.0	27,161	100.0	109.9	2.7	11.0
Treasury and Other Government	15,332	64.3	16,781	68.9	17,496	64.4	70.8	3.8	15.0
Central Bank	598	2.5	646	2.7	652	2.4	2.6	0.5	9.5
Corporate	8,790	36.9	8,884	36.5	9,012	33.2	36.5	1.0	4.1
Japan									
Total	9,078	230.8	8,853	228.4	9,326	100.0	226.7	0.5	1.8
Treasury and Other Government	8,376	213.0	8,154	210.3	8,593	92.1	208.9	0.5	1.6
Central Bank	25	0.6	20	0.5	21	0.2	0.5	(2.7)	(17.2)
Corporate	677	17.2	678	17.5	712	7.6	17.3	0.1	4.2

( ) = negative, – = not applicable, GDP = gross domestic product, Q1 = first quarter, Q4 = fourth quarter, q-o-q = quarter-on-quarter, USD = United States dollar, y-o-y = year-on-year.

Notes:

1. Emerging East Asia is defined to include ASEAN plus the People's Republic of China; Hong Kong, China; and the Republic of Korea.
2. For Singapore, corporate bonds outstanding are based on *AsianBondsOnline* estimates. For Indonesia, Q1 2025 data are based on *AsianBondsOnline* estimates.
3. Growth rates are calculated from a local currency base and do not include currency effects. For emerging East Asia, growth figures are based on 31 March 2025 currency exchange rates and do not include currency effects.
4. GDP data are from CEIC Data Company.
5. Bloomberg LP end-of-period local currency–USD rates are used.

Sources: People's Republic of China (CEIC Data Company); Hong Kong, China (Hong Kong Monetary Authority); Indonesia (Bank Indonesia; Directorate General of Budget Financing and Risk Management, Ministry of Finance; and Indonesia Stock Exchange); Japan (Japan Securities Dealers Association); Republic of Korea (Bank of Korea and KG Zeroin Corporation); Malaysia (Bank Negara Malaysia); Philippines (Bangko Sentral ng Pilipinas, Bureau of the Treasury, and Bloomberg LP); Singapore (Monetary Authority of Singapore and Bloomberg LP); Thailand (Bank of Thailand); and Viet Nam (Hanoi Stock Exchange, State Bank of Vietnam, Vietnam Bond Market Association, and Bloomberg LP).

Table A2: Local-Currency-Denominated Bond Issuance

	Q1 2024		Q4 2024		Q1 2025		Growth Rate (%)	
							Q1 2025	
	Amount (USD billion)	% share	Amount (USD billion)	% share	Amount (USD billion)	% share	q-o-q	y-o-y
People's Republic of China								
Total	1,335	100.0	1,652	100.0	1,652	100.0	(0.6)	24.4
Treasury and Other Government	703	52.7	953	57.7	1,019	61.7	6.3	45.7
Central Bank	0	0.0	0	0.0	0	0.0	–	–
Corporate	632	47.3	699	42.3	633	38.3	(9.9)	0.7
Hong Kong, China								
Total	162	100.0	181	100.0	180	100.0	(0.3)	10.4
Treasury and Other Government	0.7	0.4	11	5.9	1	0.5	(91.0)	36.4
Central Bank	128	79.1	134	74.3	135	74.8	0.4	4.4
Corporate	33	20.5	36	19.8	44	24.7	24.1	33.1
Indonesia								
Total	43	100.0	46	100.0	39	100.0	(13.2)	(5.8)
Treasury and Other Government	16	37.6	14	31.6	16	40.7	11.8	1.9
Central Bank	25	58.6	28	61.5	20	52.2	(26.4)	(16.1)
Corporate	2	3.8	3	6.9	3	7.1	(10.5)	79.0
Republic of Korea								
Total	193	100.0	194	100.0	169	100.0	(12.5)	(4.0)
Treasury and Other Government	43	22.4	28	14.4	50	29.6	79.5	26.6
Central Bank	18	9.3	14	7.4	15	8.8	4.6	(9.2)
Corporate	132	68.2	151	78.2	104	61.6	(31.0)	(13.4)
Malaysia								
Total	29	100.0	18	100.0	22	100.0	23.9	(26.1)
Treasury and Other Government	11	37.1	7	39.2	12	51.7	63.5	3.0
Central Bank	10	36.4	0	0.0	0	0.0	–	(100.0)
Corporate	8	26.5	11	60.8	11	48.3	(1.6)	34.6
Philippines								
Total	56	100.0	41	100.0	47	100.0	13.7	(14.0)
Treasury and Other Government	22	39.9	7	17.7	15	30.9	98.8	(33.3)
Central Bank	32	57.8	33	79.7	31	66.3	(5.4)	(1.3)
Corporate	1	2.3	1	2.6	1	2.7	20.6	(0.1)
Singapore								
Total	340	100.0	411	100.0	421	100.0	0.7	23.1
Treasury and Other Government	37	10.7	40	9.8	41	9.7	0.2	11.5
Central Bank	301	88.4	367	89.4	377	89.5	0.8	24.6
Corporate	3	0.9	3	0.8	3	0.8	(2.0)	16.7
Thailand								
Total	61	100.0	61	100.0	63	100.0	2.4	(4.2)
Treasury and Other Government	18	29.4	18	29.0	18	28.4	0.2	(7.7)
Central Bank	32	52.1	33	54.4	35	55.8	5.0	2.6
Corporate	11	18.5	10	16.6	10	15.9	(2.5)	(17.8)
Viet Nam								
Total	11	100.0	37	100.0	49	100.0	33.0	346.6
Treasury and Other Government	3	28.9	2	6.3	4	8.9	88.1	37.7
Central Bank	7	63.8	30	82.7	44	89.8	44.5	528.6
Corporate	0.8	7.3	4	11.0	0.6	1.3	(84.2)	(20.2)
Emerging East Asia								
Total	2,229	100.0	2,639	100.0	2,642	100.0	(0.5)	19.4
Treasury and Other Government	853	38.3	1,080	40.9	1,175	44.5	8.1	38.6
Central Bank	554	24.8	640	24.3	656	24.8	1.6	18.1
Corporate	822	36.9	919	34.8	811	30.7	(12.1)	0.2
Japan								
Total	371	100.0	340	100.0	346	100.0	(2.9)	(7.5)
Treasury and Other Government	351	94.6	301	88.6	329	94.9	4.1	(7.2)
Central Bank	0	0.0	11	3.2	0	0.0	(100.0)	–
Corporate	20	5.4	28	8.2	18	5.1	(39.8)	(12.8)

( ) = negative, – = not applicable, Q1 = first quarter, Q4 = fourth quarter, q-o-q = quarter-on-quarter, USD = United States dollar, y-o-y = year-on-year.

Notes:

1. Data reflect gross bond issuance.
2. Bloomberg LP end-of-period local currency–USD rates are used.
3. Growth rates are calculated from a local currency base and do not include currency effects. For emerging East Asia, growth figures are based on 31 March 2025 currency exchange rates and do not include currency effects.

Sources: People's Republic of China (CEIC Data Company); Hong Kong, China (Hong Kong Monetary Authority); Indonesia (Bank Indonesia, Directorate General of Budget Financing and Risk Management, Ministry of Finance; and Indonesia Stock Exchange); Japan (Japan Securities Dealers Association); Republic of Korea (Bank of Korea and KG Zeroin Corporation); Malaysia (Bank Negara Malaysia); Philippines (Bangko Sentral ng Pilipinas, Bureau of the Treasury, and Bloomberg LP); Singapore (Monetary Authority of Singapore and Bloomberg LP); Thailand (Bank of Thailand and Thai Bond Market Association); and Viet Nam (Hanoi Stock Exchange, State Bank of Vietnam, Vietnam Bond Market Association, and Bloomberg LP).

Recent Developments in the ASEAN+3 Sustainable Bond Market

Sustainable Bonds Outstanding

ASEAN+3's sustainable bond market reached a size of USD922.7 billion at the end of March on slowing growth in the first quarter (Q1) of 2025 as investment appetite soured amid heightened global uncertainties.[8] Quarter-on-quarter (q-o-q) growth moderated to 0.3% in Q1 2025 from 2.9% in the fourth quarter of 2024 due to a slowdown in issuance alongside a high volume of maturities. The sustainable bond market in ASEAN+3 grew faster than that of the United States (–0.3% q-o-q) but lagged the 2.9% q-o-q expansion of the European Union 20 (EU-20). The faster expansion of the EU-20's sustainable bond stock was buoyed by increased issuance that was supported by the continued monetary easing of the European Central Bank. ASEAN+3's sustainable bond market remained the world's second-largest regional market, accounting for 18.3% of the global sustainable bond stock at the end of Q1 2025, trailing the EU-20's global share (36.6%) but exceeding that of the United States (5.8%) (**Figure 9**). ASEAN+3's sustainable bond market comprises only 2.3% of its total bond market, compared with the EU-20's corresponding share of 8.3%. Within ASEAN+3, the People's Republic of China (PRC) has the largest sustainable bond market, accounting for 39.8% of the regional sustainable bond stock. This share, however, is smaller than the PRC's corresponding share of 56.8% in the ASEAN+3 general bond market. Meanwhile, member states of the Association of Southeast Asian Nations (ASEAN) accounted for 10.4% of the ASEAN+3 sustainable bond market, exceeding their corresponding share of 6.0% in the ASEAN+3 general bond market. Similarly, the regional sustainable bond market shares of the Republic of Korea (19.8%) and Hong Kong, China (5.1%) were also higher than their respective general bond market shares of 5.5% and 0.6%.

Figure 9: Global Sustainable Bonds Outstanding

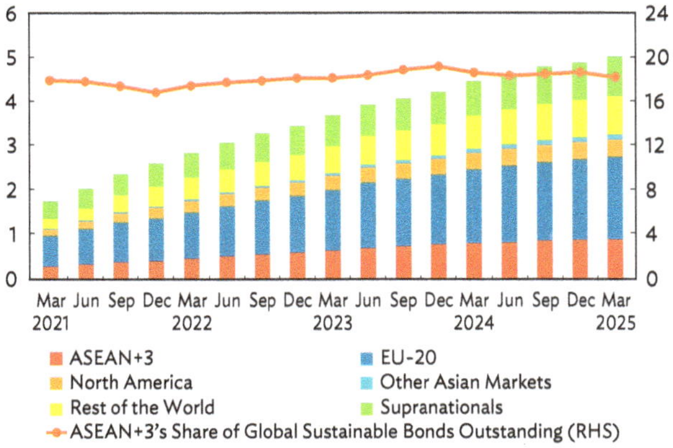

ASEAN+3 = Association of Southeast Asian Nations plus the People's Republic of China; Hong Kong, China; Japan; and the Republic of Korea; EU-20 = European Union 20; RHS = right-hand side; USD = United States dollar.

Notes:

1. The EU-20 includes EU member markets Austria, Belgium, Croatia, Cyprus, Estonia, Finland, France, Germany, Greece, Ireland, Italy, Latvia, Lithuania, Luxembourg, Malta, the Netherlands, Portugal, Slovakia, Slovenia, and Spain.
2. Data include both local currency and foreign currency issues.

Source: *AsianBondsOnline* calculations based on Bloomberg LP data.

Figure 10: Market Profile of Outstanding ASEAN+3 Sustainable Bonds at the End of March 2025

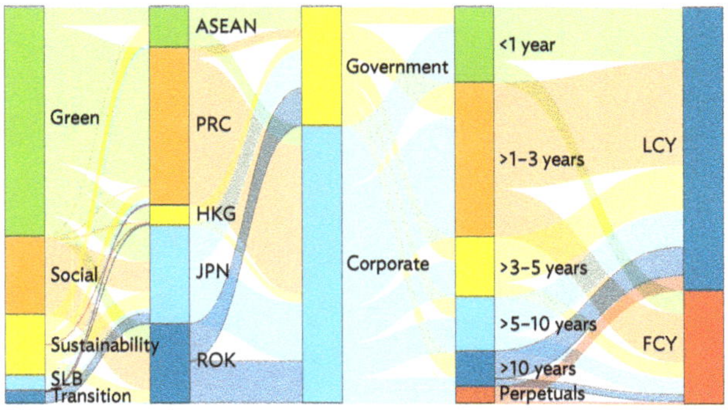

ASEAN = Association of Southeast Asian Nations; PRC = People's Republic of China; FCY = foreign currency; HKG = Hong Kong, China; JPN = Japan; ROK = Republic of Korea; LCY = local currency; SLB = sustainability-linked bond.

Notes:

1. ASEAN+3 is defined to include member states of ASEAN plus the People's Republic of China; Hong Kong, China; Japan; and the Republic of Korea.
2. ASEAN comprises the markets of Cambodia, Indonesia, the Lao People's Democratic Republic, Malaysia, the Philippines, Singapore, Thailand, and Viet Nam.
3. SLBs include transition-linked bonds.

Source: *AsianBondsOnline* calculations based on Bloomberg LP data.

---

8 ASEAN+3 comprises the member states of the Association of Southeast Asian Nations (ASEAN) plus the People's Republic of China; Hong Kong, China; Japan; and the Republic of Korea..

ASEAN+3's sustainable bond market was more diversified in Q1 2025 than the EU-20's in terms of different types of bond instruments. Green bonds accounted for 58.1% of ASEAN+3's sustainable bond stock at the end of March, followed by social bonds (19.6%) and sustainability bonds (15.2%) (**Figure 10**). The market shares of social bonds, sustainability bonds, and transition bonds are all higher in ASEAN+3 than in the EU-20. As measured by the Herfindahl–Hirschman Index, a gauge used to reflect the concentration of certain bond types within a market, ASEAN+3 has a lower score than the EU-20, suggesting greater diversity in terms of bond instruments in the ASEAN+3 market (**Table**). Private sector issuance accounted for 69.6% of sustainable bonds outstanding in the ASEAN+3 market at the end of Q1 2025, which exceeded the corresponding shares of 24.0% in the ASEAN+3 general bond market and 51.1% in the EU-20 sustainable bond market. Among ASEAN+3 markets, the private sector's share of sustainable bonds outstanding at the end of March was the largest in the PRC (93.6%), Japan (59.6%), and the Republic of Korea (52.6%). In contrast, the public sector is more active in the sustainable bond markets of Hong Kong, China (58.2%) and ASEAN member states (52.5%). Meanwhile, the local currency (LCY) financing share rose to 71.5% in ASEAN+3's sustainable bond market in Q1 2025 from 69.8% a year earlier. However, this was still less than the EU-20's LCY financing share of 89.9%.

Table: Instrument, Issuer, and Currency Profiles in the ASEAN+3 and European Union 20 Sustainable Bond Markets at the End of March 2025

By End-March 2025	ASEAN+3	EU-20
Instrument profile (as a share of regional sustainable bonds outstanding)		
Green bonds	58.1%	65.3%
Social bonds	19.6%	17.4%
Sustainability bonds	15.2%	9.3%
SLBs (including transition-linked bonds)	4.0%	7.8%
Transition bonds	3.2%	0.3%
Herfindahl–Hirschman Index (based on shares of each bond type)	0.40	0.47
Issuer and currency profile		
Private sector (as a share of regional general bonds outstanding)	24.0%	39.5%
Private sector (as a share of regional sustainable bonds outstanding)	69.6%	51.1%
LCY financing (as a share of regional general bonds outstanding)	95.4%	89.5%
LCY financing (as a share of regional sustainable bonds outstanding)	71.5%	89.9%

ASEAN+3 = Association of Southeast Asian Nations plus the People's Republic of China; Hong Kong, China; Japan; and the Republic of Korea; EU-20 = European Union 20; LCY = local currency; SLB = sustainability-linked bond.

Note: The EU-20 includes European Union member markets Austria, Belgium, Croatia, Cyprus, Estonia, Finland, France, Germany, Greece, Ireland, Italy, Latvia, Lithuania, Luxembourg, Malta, the Netherlands, Portugal, Slovakia, Slovenia, and Spain.

Source: *AsianBondsOnline* calculations based on Bloomberg LP data.

A majority of the sustainable bonds outstanding in ASEAN+3 at the end of Q1 2025 comprised short- to medium-term financing. Among sustainable bonds outstanding in the ASEAN+3 market at the end of March, 73.2% carried remaining tenors of 5 years or less, compared with 49.8% in the EU-20 sustainable bond market (**Figure 11**). The size-weighted average tenor of the ASEAN+3 sustainable bond stock stood at 4.5 years at the end of March versus 7.5 years for the EU-20. Within ASEAN+3, ASEAN markets have a relatively higher share of sustainable bonds in longer tenors,

Figure 11: Tenor Profiles of ASEAN+3 and European Union 20 Sustainable Bonds Outstanding at the End of March 2025

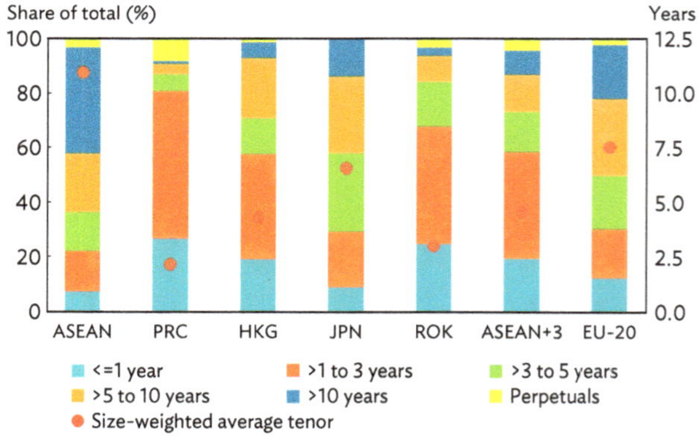

ASEAN = Association of Southeast Asian Nations; PRC = People's Republic of China; EU-20 = European Union 20; HKG = Hong Kong, China; JPN = Japan; ROK = Republic of Korea.

Notes:

1. ASEAN+3 is defined to include member states of ASEAN plus the People's Republic of China; Hong Kong, China; Japan; and the Republic of Korea.
2. ASEAN comprises the markets of Cambodia, Indonesia, the Lao People's Democratic Republic, Malaysia, the Philippines, Singapore, Thailand, and Viet Nam.
3. The EU-20 includes European Union member markets Austria, Belgium, Croatia, Cyprus, Estonia, Finland, France, Germany, Greece, Ireland, Italy, Latvia, Lithuania, Luxembourg, Malta, the Netherlands, Portugal, Slovakia, Slovenia, and Spain.
4. Data include both local currency and foreign currency issues.

Source: *AsianBondsOnline* calculations based on Bloomberg LP data.

with 63.6% of outstanding sustainable bonds carrying remaining tenors of over 5 years, resulting in a size-weighted average tenor of 11.0 years. Among individual ASEAN markets, the size-weighted average tenor was the longest in Singapore (16.2 years) and the Philippines (12.6 years). In the ASEAN+3 sustainable bond market, bonds issued by the public sector tend to have longer maturities. The governments of Indonesia, Singapore, and Thailand have regularly issued sovereign sustainable bonds, with relatively long maturities as part of their Treasury auctions. Their cumulative issuance from Q1 2019 through Q1 2025 carried a size-weighted average maturity of 21.8 years. By bond type, over 70% of outstanding social bonds and green bonds in ASEAN+3 had remaining tenors of 5 years or less at the end of March (**Figure 12**).

Figure 12: Tenor Profiles of ASEAN+3 and European Union 20 Sustainable Bonds Outstanding by Type of Bond at the End of March 2025

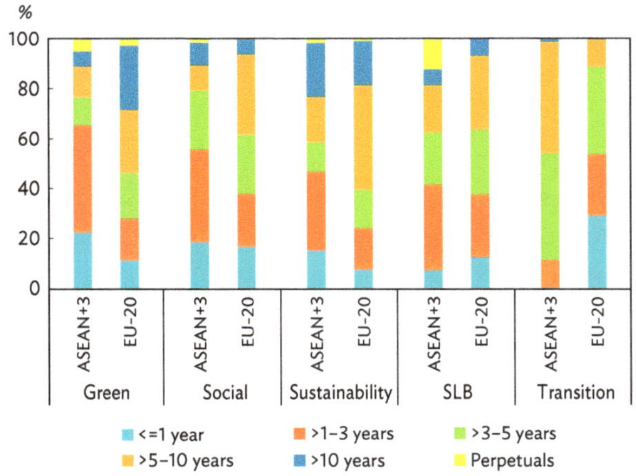

ASEAN+3 = Association of Southeast Asian Nations plus the People's Republic of China; Hong Kong, China; Japan; and the Republic of Korea; EU-20 = European Union 20; SLB = sustainability-linked bond.

Notes:

1. The EU-20 includes EU member markets Austria, Belgium, Croatia, Cyprus, Estonia, Finland, France, Germany, Greece, Ireland, Italy, Latvia, Lithuania, Luxembourg, Malta, the Netherlands, Portugal, Slovakia, Slovenia, and Spain.
2. Data include both local currency and foreign currency issues.
3. SLBs include transition-linked bonds.

Source: *AsianBondsOnline* computations based on Bloomberg LP data.

Sustainable Bond Issuance

Sustainable bond issuance in ASEAN+3 contracted 24.0% q-o-q to USD47.7 billion in Q1 2025, the lowest quarterly issuance total of the past 4 years, amid heightened global uncertainties. ASEAN+3's sustainable bond issuance as a share of the global total fell to 21.0% in Q1 2025, making it the third-largest issuer of sustainable bonds globally during the quarter after the EU-20 (28.6%) and supranationals (29.2%). The issuance of all sustainable bond types in ASEAN+3 declined during the quarter except for transition bonds (**Figure 13**). By economy, the PRC accounted for 55.2% of ASEAN+3's total quarterly issuance of sustainable bonds, with its green bond issuance representing 82.3% of the regional total in Q1 2025. ASEAN members collectively accounted for 9.0% of ASEAN+3's quarterly issuance total, up from 8.3% in the previous quarter, and were the region's leading issuers of sustainability bonds with 36.5% of the quarterly total. The Republic of Korea led the region in the issuance of social bonds in Q1 2025 (69.5% of regional social bond issuance), while Japan led in the issuance of sustainability-linked bonds (53.0.%) and transition bonds (77.4%).

Figure 13: ASEAN+3 Sustainable Bond Issuance and Share of the Global Total

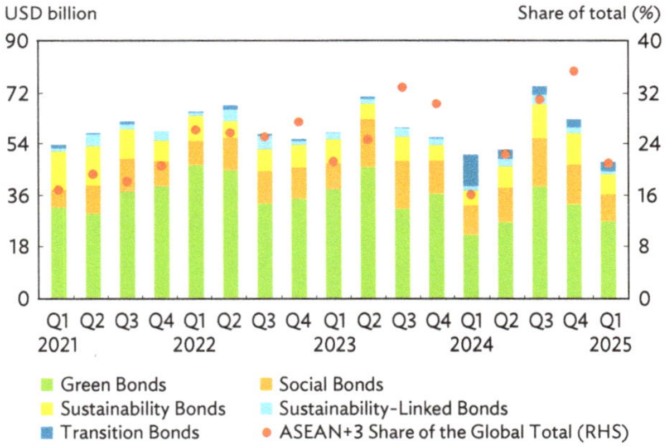

ASEAN+3 = Association of Southeast Asian Nations plus the People's Republic of China; Hong Kong, China; Japan; and the Republic of Korea; RHS = right-hand side; USD = United States dollar.

Notes:

1. Data include both local currency and foreign currency issues.
2. Sustainability-linked bonds include transition-linked bonds.

Source: *AsianBondsOnline* calculations based on Bloomberg LP data.

ASEAN+3 sustainable bond issuance in Q1 2025 included less LCY financing and long-term financing compared to issuances in 2024 (Figure 14).

- LCY-denominated bonds comprised 72.9% of total ASEAN+3 sustainable bond issuance in Q1 2025, which was down from 75.8% in full-year 2024. This was much lower than the 94.3% share of LCY financing in ASEAN+3's general bond market issuance in

Figure 14: Market Profile of ASEAN+3 Sustainable Bond Issuance in the First Quarter of 2025

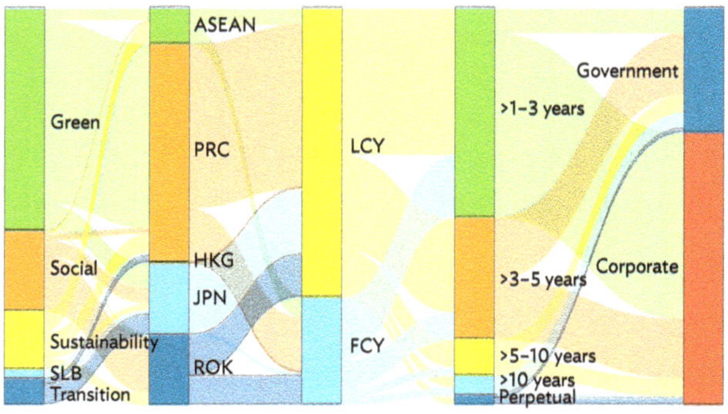

ASEAN = Association of Southeast Asian Nations; PRC = People's Republic of China; FCY = foreign currency; HKG = Hong Kong, China; JPN = Japan; ROK = Republic of Korea; LCY = local currency; SLB = sustainability-linked bond.

Notes:
1. ASEAN+3 is defined to include member states of ASEAN plus the People's Republic of China; Hong Kong, China; Japan; and the Republic of Korea.
2. ASEAN comprises the markets of Cambodia, Indonesia, Malaysia, the Philippines, Singapore, Thailand, and Viet Nam.
3. SLBs include transition-linked bonds.

Source: *AsianBondsOnline* calculations based on Bloomberg LP data.

Figure 15: ASEAN+3 Sustainable Bond Issuance by Sector in the First Quarter of 2025

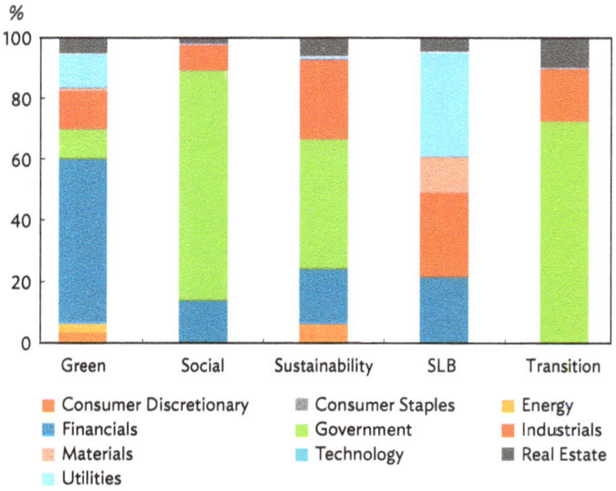

SLB = sustainability-linked bond.

Notes:
1. ASEAN+3 is defined to include member states of the Association of Southeast Asian Nations plus the People's Republic of China; Hong Kong, China; Japan; and the Republic of Korea.
2. Data include both local currency and foreign currency issues.
3. SLBs include transition-linked bonds.

Source: *AsianBondsOnline* computations based on Bloomberg LP data.

Q1 2025. In ASEAN, the average LCY financing share in members' sustainable bond markets was 44.6%, which was well below the average share of 70.9% in their general bond markets. Among ASEAN+3 markets, only Japan saw comparable LCY financing shares in its sustainable (94.0%) and general (90.8%) bond markets in Q1 2025. In the EU-20, LCY financing shares were also comparable in the sustainable (82.2%) and general (87.7%) bond markets.

- Around 83.4% of ASEAN+3 sustainable bond issuance in Q1 2025 carried maturities of 5 years or less, up from 73.5% in full-year 2024. Sustainable bond issuances with maturities of 5 years or less dominated in Hong Kong, China (100%); the PRC (94.3%); and the Republic of Korea (93.7%) in Q1 2025. In ASEAN, the corresponding share was much lower at 40.1% due to active public sector issuance, which accounted for 78.9% of total ASEAN long-term sustainable bond issuance during the quarter.
- Private sector issuers accounted for 68.5% of sustainable bond issuance in ASEAN+3 in Q1 2025. This contrasts with 34.2% for ASEAN+3's general bond issuance. The private sector was more active in issuing sustainability-linked bonds (100.0%) and green bonds (90.4%) in Q1 2025, while the public sector was the larger issuer of social bonds (75.4%) and transition bonds (73.1%) (**Figure 15**). Private sector issuance in Q1 2025 was led by issuers from the financial (53.1%) and industrial (21.2%) sectors.

Policy and Regulatory Developments

People's Republic of China

The People's Bank of China Reduces Reserve Requirement Ratio and Unveils Other Economic Support Measures

On 7 May, the People's Bank of China announced that it would reduce the reserve requirement ratio by 50 basis points (bps) to 9.0%, effective 15 May. In addition, it said that it would raise by CNY300 billion the relending facility available to technology companies and establish a CNY500 billion relending facility for services consumption and elderly care. The central bank also reduced by 25 bps the rate charged on its housing provident loan fund.

The People's Bank of China and China Securities Regulatory Commission Release Rules for Innovation Bonds

On 7 May, the People's Bank of China and the China Securities Regulatory Commission announced rules to facilitate the issuance of innovation bonds. The measures include supporting equity investment institutions such as financial institutions and private equity companies; encouraging issuers to issue longer-term bonds; streamlining the bond issuance process, including issuances as part of the government's performance appraisal of technology companies; and encouraging local governments to provide support such as guarantees.

Hong Kong, China

Hong Kong Monetary Authority Announces Bond Issuance for the Second and Third Quarters

On 17 April, the Hong Kong Monetary Authority published the tentative issuance schedule for Hong Kong Special Administrative Region Institutional Government Bonds under the Institutional Bond Programme and Government Sustainable Bond Programme for the second and third quarters of 2025. In the second quarter, HKD9.5 billion of local currency bonds with maturities of 1–15 years will be issued and CNY5.5 billion worth of bonds denominated in Chinese yuan with maturities of 1–10 years will also be auctioned. In the third quarter, the tentative amount of HKD-denominated bonds to be issued will total HKD6.75 billion, while the amount of CNY-denominated bonds to be offered will total CNY7.75 billion. The HKD-denominated bonds will carry maturities of 1–20 years, while the CNY-denominated bonds will have maturities of 1–10 years.

Indonesia

Indonesia Concludes Debt Switch

In February, the Government of Indonesia conducted a debt switch amounting to IDR502.0 billion versus total bids worth IDR1,344.0 billion. The eligible bonds for the debt switch included 15 series of Treasury bonds with varying maturities covering the period 2025–2029. The destination bonds comprised six series that will mature from 2030 to 2064. The government will offer another debt exchange in August.

Republic of Korea

The Government of the Republic of Korea Approves First Supplementary Budget for 2025

On 18 April, the government approved the first supplementary budget proposal for 2025 worth KRW12.2 trillion. The proposal comprised KRW3.2 trillion allotted for disaster and emergency response, KRW4.4 trillion for trade enhancement and artificial intelligence competitiveness, KRW4.3 trillion to support people's livelihood, and KRW0.2 trillion for other government projects. Subsequently, on 1 May, the National Assembly approved the supplementary budget at an increased amount of KRW13.8 trillion.

Ministry of Economy and Finance Announces Adjusted Korea Treasury Bond Issuance Plan for 2025

On 7 May, the Ministry of Economy and Finance (MOEF) announced adjustments to its Korea Treasury Bond issuance plan for 2025 to reflect the approved supplementary budget. The issuance ceiling was raised to KRW207.1 trillion from KRW197.6 trillion. The MOEF will continue with its schedule of issuing 55%–60% of the total volume in the first half of the year, and the remaining 40%–45% in the second half. In terms of tenors, the MOEF is planning to maintain the share of short-term bonds (2 years and 3 years) at 30±3%, reduce the share of medium-term bonds (5 years and 10 years) to 30±3% from 35±3%, and increase that of long-term bonds (20–50 years) to 40±5% from 35±5%.

Malaysia

Bank Negara Malaysia Reduces Statutory Reserve Requirement Ratio

On 8 May, Bank Negara Malaysia reduced the statutory reserve requirement ratio by 100 bps from 2.0% to 1.0%, the lowest it has been in 14 years, effective 16 May. This decision was made to ensure financial market stability amid uncertainties, along with promoting financial intermediation activities. The statutory reserve requirement ratio reduction will free up about MYR19 billion of funds in the financial market.

Philippines

Bangko Sentral ng Pilipinas Expands Trust Entities' Access to Central Bank Securities

On 15 January, the Bangko Sentral ng Pilipinas (BSP) issued Circular No. 1207 which allows trust entities to invest in BSP securities via Investment Management Accounts alongside Unit Investment Trust Funds. This amendment also covers secondary market trading via the Philippine Dealing and Exchange Corporation. The expanded access aims to boost the tradability and liquidity of BSP securities, enhance the BSP's capacity to absorb excess cash in the financial system, and improve monetary policy transmission.

Singapore

Singapore's Parliament Passes 2025 Budget Spending Plan

On 10 March, the Singapore Parliament approved a 2025 budget spending plan totaling SGD143.1 billion, equivalent to 18.7% of Singapore's gross domestic product, up from SGD134.2 billion spent in 2024. The approved budget is in line with projected government spending targeted to reach about 20.0% of gross domestic product by 2030. State revenue is projected to reach SGD122.8 billion in 2025 and will be supported by collections from corporate and personal income taxes, the goods and services tax, and carbon taxes, among others.

Thailand

Public Debt Management Office Conducts THB25 Billion Bond Switch

On 21 February, the Public Debt Management Office concluded bond switch transactions totaling THB25.0 billion, the second series of such transactions for fiscal year 2025. The transactions allowed investors to swap their holdings of the designated source bonds, which were maturing shortly, with designated destination bonds that have longer remaining tenors. The source bond for this batch of bond switch carried tenors of less than 1 year, while tenors of the six destination bonds ranged from 4.7 years to 47.3 years. The bond switch is part of the Public Debt Management Office's fundraising program for fiscal year 2025 and supports its debt management objectives by reducing the bunching of short-term debt and increasing the liquidity of 5- to 50-year government bonds.

Viet Nam

Viet Nam Plans to Auction VND120.0 Trillion Worth of Government Bonds in the Second Quarter of 2025

The Government of Viet Nam plans to raise VND120.0 trillion in the second quarter of 2025 through its Treasury bond offering. The planned issuance represents 24.0% of the total VND500.0 trillion auction plan for 2025 and was 8.1% higher than the VND111.0 trillion auction plan in the previous quarter. The Treasury bonds to be auctioned will carry maturities of 5–30 years with auctions to be scheduled every Wednesday.

Unveiled by Deep Learning: The Environmental, Social, and Governance Emphasis of Leading Companies in East Asia and Southeast Asia

Investors are increasingly looking at available information on environmental sustainability, social responsibility, and governance quality for guidance to evaluate corporate performances. Environmental, social, and governance (ESG) factors have become critical components of corporate strategy and reporting. Yet, understanding the emphasis that different companies place on these topics—especially across multilingual, multicultural environments—remains limited.

According to the European Commission (2022), while many market participants use ESG ratings, they also believe that the ESG ratings market does not function well. They consider the lack of transparency and presence of bias in ratings methodologies to be problematic, which leads to low correlation among various ESG ratings.

An Asian Development Bank working paper by Li et al. (forthcoming) investigates how the largest companies in eight East Asian and Southeast Asian economies address ESG issues in their corporate reports. The study addresses the gap in ESG reporting by analyzing large-scale unstructured text data using advanced natural language processing tools and artificial intelligence (AI).

Utilizing a sophisticated AI and deep learning model—the Text Match Pre-Trained Transformer (TMPT)—the authors analyze 480 annual and integrated reports from 293 listed companies with the largest market capitalizations in the stock markets of the People's Republic of China (PRC), Japan, the Republic of Korea, Indonesia, Malaysia, the Philippines, Singapore, and Thailand. The 2023 annual reports (published in 2024) were gathered in both English and the respective local language when available. Thirteen ESG-related topics were examined, including human rights, work environment, governance risk, and greenhouse gas emissions. This enabled a detailed examination of ESG disclosure patterns and regional variation.

The TMPT was trained using huge amounts of text from Wikipedia and academic research in multiple languages. This advanced AI model works by comparing company reports with a list of 13 ESG topics—like climate change, human rights, and job creation—to see how closely the company's words match each topic. Every report was broken into small sections, and the model checked how much each section discussed these issues. It then gave every company a score showing how much it focused on each ESG topic. The TMPT model offers a scalable, multilingual approach for detecting ESG content without relying on predefined taxonomies, enabling more consistent comparisons across linguistic and national contexts. Importantly, the study finds substantial differences in ESG emphasis among economies, shaped by their unique regulatory environments, cultural contexts, and economic conditions.

This powerful AI tool—with over 519 million adjustable settings—performed very well, correctly identifying ESG content about 90% of the time. It worked best in languages where more training data were available such as English, Chinese, and Japanese.

The paper builds on prior work by Yoshida et al. (2024), who questioned the consistency and reliability of conventional ESG ratings. In contrast, the approach of Li et al. (forthcoming) enables a nuanced assessment of ESG-related discourse without imposing a rigid, one-size-fits-all scoring system. Another key contribution of this study is its analysis of language-based disclosure differences. Reports written in Japanese, Chinese, and Korean show strong alignment with their English counterparts, whereas discrepancies are more pronounced in Thai and Bahasa Indonesia, pointing to possible challenges in ESG-related vocabulary and reporting standards.

This special section was written by Satoru Yamadera (advisor) at the Economic Research and Development Impact Department of the Asian Development Bank and Shunsuke Managi (distinguished professor and director) of the Urban Institute at the Department of Civil Engineering at Kyushu University.

Li et al. (forthcoming) find that top companies in the Republic of Korea place greater emphasis on environmental and social topics, while leading companies in the PRC focus more on economic dimensions. Top Japanese firms balance various ESG topics, notably emphasizing work environment and domestic job creation. Meanwhile, leading companies in Indonesia, Malaysia, and the Philippines give relatively more attention to community-related and human rights issues.

Key Findings

Overall Environmental, Social, and Governance Emphasis Patterns

Across all reviewed reports, companies emphasized economic and governance topics—particularly economic ripple effects, production costs, and governance risks—more than social or environmental ones. Social topics like domestic job creation and work environment were also notable. Environmental topics such as mining, consumption, and greenhouse gases received moderate attention (**Figure 16**).

People's Republic of China. Reports in the PRC had a strong focus on economic topics (e.g., ripple effects, production costs). This aligns with the PRC's focus on post-COVID-19 economic recovery in 2023.

Republic of Korea. Reports from the Republic of Korea placed the most emphasis on environmental and social topics, such as work environment and greenhouse gas emissions, although there was large intra-market variance.

Japan. Japanese reports reflected a balanced focus, with the most emphasis on social aspects like job creation and work environment.

Indonesia, Malaysia, and the Philippines. Among these three economies, reports generally gave greater emphasis to community-related issues and human rights. Malaysia notably emphasized governance risk, while the Philippines focused more on water management.

Singapore. The focus of annual reports in Singapore leaned toward economic topics, particularly job creation.

Thailand. Reports in Thailand showed a relatively balanced profile that was close to the regional average on most topics.

Intra-Market Variance

While market-level trends are identifiable, significant variation within economies was also observed. For example, Korean companies differed greatly in how much they emphasize environmental and social issues—some heavily emphasize them, while others focus primarily on economic topics.

Language Consistency

Out of 163 companies with bilingual reports, a high degree of consistency was found in the PRC, Japan, and the Republic of Korea, indicating effective translation and standardization of ESG messaging (**Figure 17**). Reports from Thailand and Indonesia exhibited inconsistencies between their English and local language versions, possibly due to translation practices or a lack of ESG literacy in local languages. This discrepancy might also stem from the scarcity of ESG-related content in these languages, limiting the enforced training of the TMPT model.

Policy Implications

This study demonstrates the utility of AI in understanding nuanced ESG reporting patterns across languages and economies. It also underscores the influence of national priorities, regulatory environments, and cultural factors on ESG disclosures.

For instance, the emphasis of firms in the PRC on economic factors reflects the government's push for economic stability. Meanwhile, Korean firms' engagement with social and environmental themes reflects both societal pressure and the influence of large conglomerates. In contrast, community-related disclosures in Southeast Asia may reflect local development challenges.

The analysis also points to a broader concern: Disparities in ESG understanding and communication across economies may be exacerbated by the limitations of AI models trained on linguistically unequal data. This indicates a need for capacity building in ESG education and data availability in underrepresented languages.

Figure 16: Average Absolute Environmental, Social, and Governance Emphasis in Annual Corporate Reporting Among Selected East Asian and Southeast Asian Economies (%)

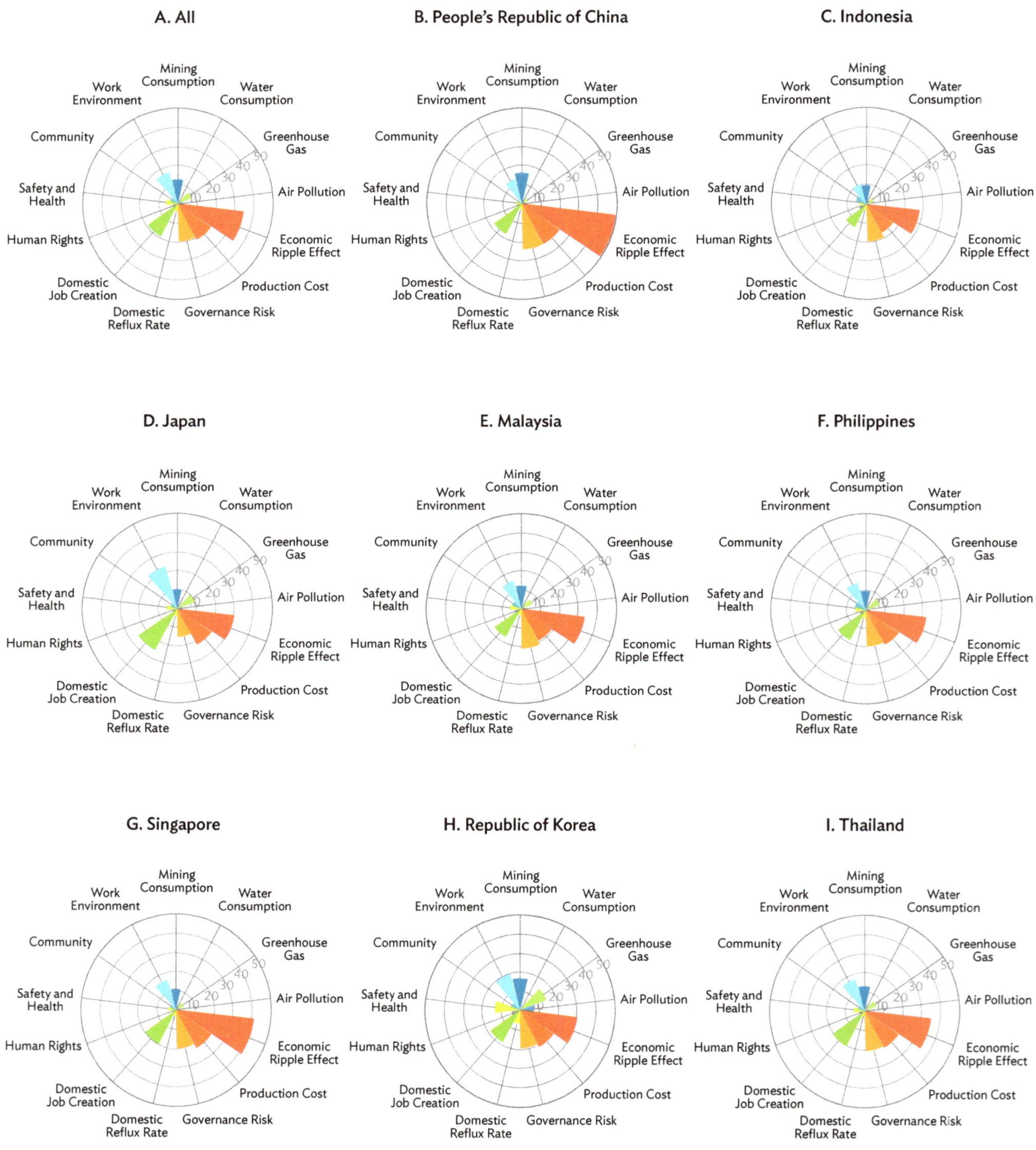

Source: Author's calculations.

Figure 17: Correlation Results of the Language Consistency Analysis

Item	People's Republic of China	Indonesia	Japan	Republic of Korea	Thailand
Air Pollution	0.63	0.97	0.57	0.44	−0.06
Greenhouse Gas	0.47	0.94	0.85	0.42	−0.18
Water Consumption	0.49	1.00	0.42	0.31	−0.21
Mining Consumption	0.66	0.85	0.60	0.22	0.12
Work Environment	0.38	0.80	0.33	0.23	0.17
Community	0.19	0.95	0.29	0.58	0.44
Safety and Health	0.31	0.81	0.63	0.72	0.62
Human Rights	0.25	0.31	0.17	0.32	0.40
Domestic Job Creation	0.22	−0.33	0.20	0.12	0.11
Domestic Reflux Rate	0.16	−0.60	0.21	0.23	0.22
Governance Risk	0.45	−0.19	0.02	0.42	−0.33
Production Cost	0.57	0.95	0.25	0.52	0.17
Economic Ripple Effect	0.59	−0.64	0.51	0.82	−0.22

1.00 0.75 0.50 0.25 0.00 −0.25 −0.50 −0.75 −1.00

Source: Author's calculations.

Overall, the study illustrates the impact of AI in improving the transparency, comparability, and contextual understanding of ESG disclosures, providing a valuable alternative to traditional single-scale evaluations. Meanwhile, stakeholder engagement through improved disclosure is fundamental for understanding companies' commitment to ESG issues. The number of integrated reports published is increasing; however, not all leading companies included in this study have issued one. Integrated reporting can enhance transparency and strengthen stakeholder engagement. Nevertheless, a key limitation is the lack of standardization and comparability across reports. This study addresses that limitation and enhances the practical value of integrated reports with narratives that explain corporate strategy. To further improve transparency and corporate governance, regulators and companies should adopt diverse communication tools, including integrated reports, and promote timely disclosure practices. The publication of integrated reports and translation to English is often seen as a challenge to small and medium-sized companies due to the costs involved. However, regardless of the form of disclosure and communication, advanced technology can provide ways to assess companies' business strategies alongside stakeholders' various environmental and social interests.

References

European Commission. 2022. *Summary Report: Targeted Consultation on the Functioning of the ESG Ratings Market in the EU and on the Consideration of ESG Factors in Credit Ratings*.

Yoshida, K., J. Xie, S. Managi, and S. Yamadera. 2024. Environmental, Social, and Governance Performance and Financial Impacts: Comparative Analysis of Companies in Asia. *ADB Working Paper Series*. No. 741. Asian Development Bank.

Li, C., A. Ryota Keeley, S. Managi, and S. Yamadera. Forthcoming. The Environmental, Social, and Governance Emphasis of Leading Companies in East Asia and Southeast Asia Unveiled by Deep Learning. *ADB Working Paper Series*. Asian Development Bank.

Market Summaries

People's Republic of China

Yield Movements

The yield curve for local currency (LCY) bonds in the People's Republic of China (PRC) shifted downward for most maturities over lingering concerns about a weakening domestic economy despite the imposition of a 90-day tariff pause between the US and the PRC. On average, bond yields fell 3 basis points (bps) across the curve from 3 March to 30 May over heightened economic uncertainties (**Figure 1**). The PRC's gross domestic product grew 5.4% year-on-year (y-o-y) in the first quarter (Q1) of 2025, the same pace as in the previous quarter, due to the government's stimulus efforts. More recent data show some weakening. Industrial production fell to 6.1% y-o-y in April from 7.7% y-o-y in March. Similarly, retail sales growth fell to 5.1% y-o-y in April from 5.9% y-o-y in March. To help the economy this year, the Government of the PRC announced a 2025 GDP growth target of 5.0% y-o-y, which was equal to the rate of growth achieved in 2024, and a higher budget deficit target of 4.0% in 2025 versus a deficit of 3.0% recorded in 2024. Also in May, the People's Bank of China reduced the 7-day reverse repurchase rate, the 1-year loan prime rate, and the 5-year loan prime rate by 10 bps each (to 1.40%, 3.00%, and 3.50%, respectively), and the reserve requirement ratio by 50 bps to 9.00%.

Figure 1: The People's Republic of China's Benchmark Yield Curve—Local Currency Government Bonds

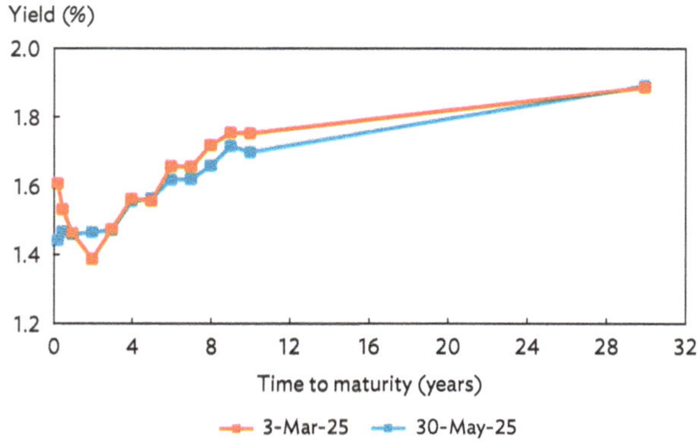

Source: Based on data from Bloomberg LP.

Local Currency Bond Market Size and Issuance

Growth in LCY bonds outstanding in the PRC slowed in Q1 2025, with the market reaching a size of CNY159.7 trillion at the end of March. LCY bonds grew 3.0% quarter-on-quarter (q-o-q) in Q1 2025, down from 3.6% q-o-q in the prior quarter (**Figure 2**). Both the government and corporate bond segments posted moderating growth in Q1 2025. For government bonds, the rate of expansion slowed to 3.9% q-o-q in Q1 2025 from 4.5% q-o-q in the previous quarter, and for corporate bonds growth slowed to 1.0% q-o-q from 1.8% q-o-q. Government bonds saw a slowdown on increased maturities, while growth in corporate bonds decelerated as companies were cautious with new issuance amid concerns over the economy.

Figure 2: Composition of Local Currency Bonds Outstanding in the People's Republic of China

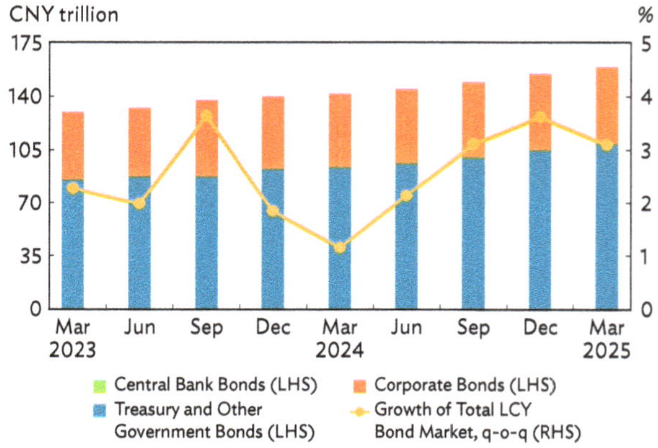

CNY = Chinese yuan, LCY = local currency, LHS = left-hand side, q-o-q = quarter-on-quarter, RHS = right-hand side.
Source: CEIC Data Company.

This market summary was written by Russ Jason Lo, consultant, Economic Research and Development Impact Department, Asian Development Bank, Manila.

The PRC's bond issuance contracted 0.6% q-o-q in Q1 2025, falling to CNY12.0 trillion. The decline in quarterly issuance was driven by the reduced issuance of corporate bonds, which fell 9.9% q-o-q to CNY4.6 trillion (**Figure 3**). Corporate bond issuance declined for the second consecutive quarter amid ongoing economic challenges in this segment of the PRC's LCY bond market. In contrast, government bond issuance grew 6.3% q-o-q to total CNY7.4 trillion. Following the 5 March parliamentary meeting, the Government of the PRC announced that it would issue an additional CNY1.3 trillion in special long-term bonds in 2025 and set a quota of CNY4.4 trillion for local government bond issuance.

Figure 3: Composition of Local Currency Bond Issuance in the People's Republic of China

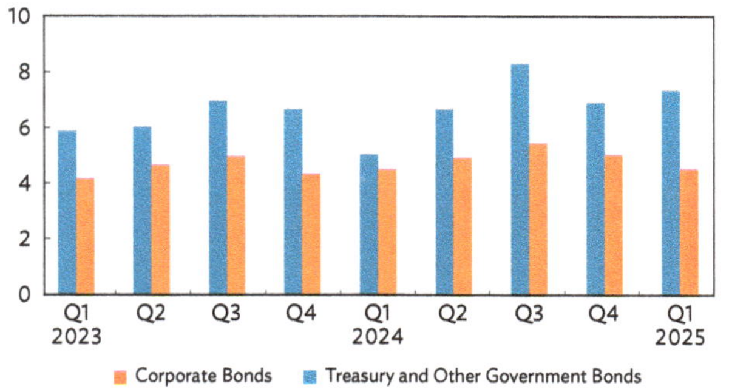

CNY = Chinese yuan, Q1 = first quarter, Q2 = second quarter, Q3 = third quarter, Q4 = fourth quarter.
Source: CEIC Data Company.

Investor Profile

Banks remained the largest holder of Treasury bonds at the end of March. However, there was a decline in the share of bank holdings to 66.7% at the end of March from 70.0% a year earlier (**Figure 4**). Part of the decline was due to central bank efforts, beginning in 2024, to reduce speculative trading. Foreign investors' holdings share declined to 6.2% from 8.7% during the same period on investor concerns over the economy. Despite the decline in banks' holding share, the PRC had the region's second-highest Herfindahl–Hirschman Index score at the end of March.[9]

Figure 4: Investor Profile of Treasury Bonds

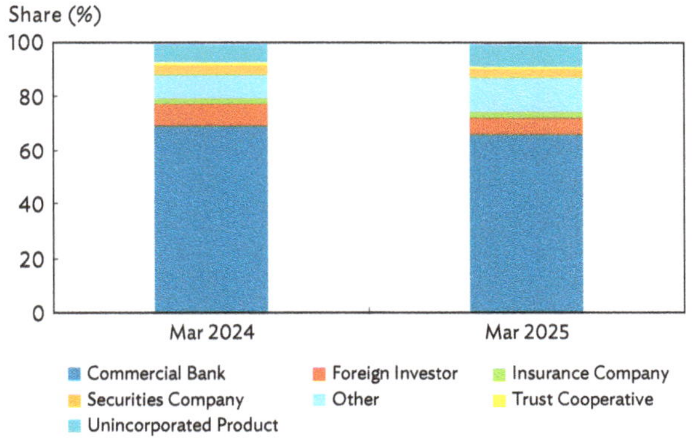

Source: CEIC Data Company.

Sustainable Bond Market

The PRC's sustainable bond market remains mostly composed of green bond instruments and private sector financing. The PRC has the largest sustainable bond market in emerging East Asia, which reached a size of USD367.4 billion and comprised 53.0% of the regional total at the end of March (**Figure 5**). A majority of the PRC's sustainable bonds are green bonds, with a share of 87.2%. The PRC bond market includes very few transition bonds and social bonds, with only 0.4% and 0.9% respective shares of its sustainable bond market. Private corporations are the most common issuer of sustainable bonds in the PRC, accounting for 93.6% of outstanding sustainable bonds, in contrast to its general bond market where the government has a 69.8% share. Finally, the majority of issuances are short term, with 87.1% of outstanding sustainable bonds having a tenor of 5 years or less.

Figure 5: Market Profile of Outstanding Sustainable Bonds in the People's Republic of China at the End of March 2025

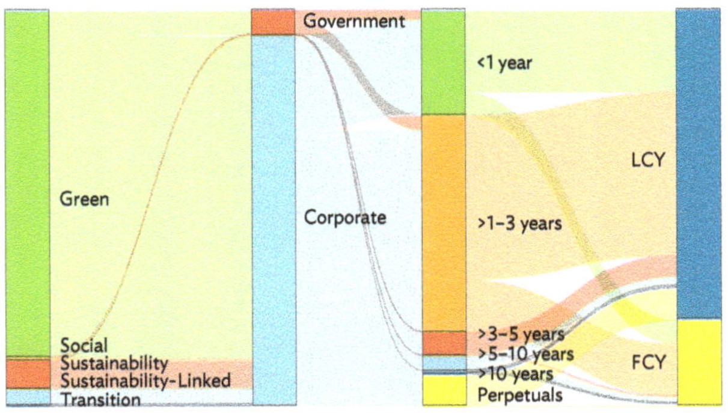

FCY = foreign currency, LCY = local currency.
Source: *AsianBondsOnline* calculations based on Bloomberg LP data.

9 The Herfindahl–Hirschman Index is a common measure of market concentration. The index is used to measure the investor profile diversification of the local currency bond market by summing the squared share of each investor group in the bond market. Emerging East Asia is defined to include member states of the Association of Southeast Asian Nations plus the People's Republic of China; Hong Kong, China; and the Republic of Korea.

Hong Kong, China

Yield Movements

Between 3 March and 30 May, local currency (LCY) government bond yields in Hong Kong, China fell across all maturities. Bond yields declined an average of 156 basis points amid heightened uncertainty linked to ongoing global trade tensions that pose downside risks to the domestic economy's near-term growth outlook (**Figure 1**). Hong Kong, China's economy expanded 3.1% year-on-year in the first quarter (Q1) of 2025, up from 2.5% year-on-year in the previous quarter. Nonetheless, economic activity has shown signs of weakening. The Purchasing Managers Index contracted for 4 consecutive months, inching up to 49.0 in May after edging down to 48.3 in March and April from 49.0 in February. The fall in Hong Kong, China's bond yields was more pronounced compared with its regional peers after the Hong Kong Monetary Authority in early May increased the supply of Hong Kong dollars in the financial system, exerting additional downward pressure on interest rates.

Figure 1: Hong Kong, China's Benchmark Yield Curve—Local Currency Government Bonds

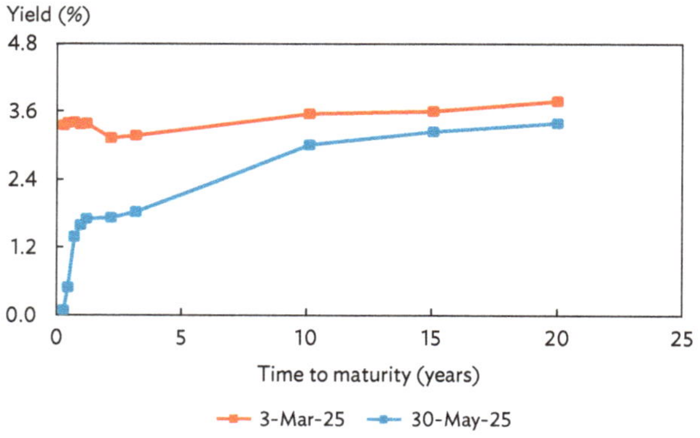

Source: Based on data from Bloomberg LP.

Local Currency Bond Market Size and Issuance

Growth in Hong Kong, China's LCY bond market eased in Q1 2025 due to the weaker expansion of Hong Kong Special Administrative Region (HKSAR) government bonds. Outstanding LCY bonds totaled HKD3,246.2 billion at the end of March, rising 3.8% quarter-on-quarter (q-o-q) in Q1 2025 versus 4.9% q-o-q in the fourth quarter (Q4) of 2024 (**Figure 2**). The slower growth in Q1 2025 than in Q4 2024 was largely driven by weaker growth of HKSAR government bonds (1.8% q-o-q versus 36.6% q-o-q) due to reduced issuance. Meanwhile, the pace of expansion in the corporate bond stock picked up, rising to 6.6% q-o-q in Q1 2025 from 3.5% q-o-q in Q4 2024. Growth in Exchange Fund Bills and Notes was steady at 0.9% q-o-q in both quarters.

Figure 2: Composition of Local Currency Bonds Outstanding in Hong Kong, China

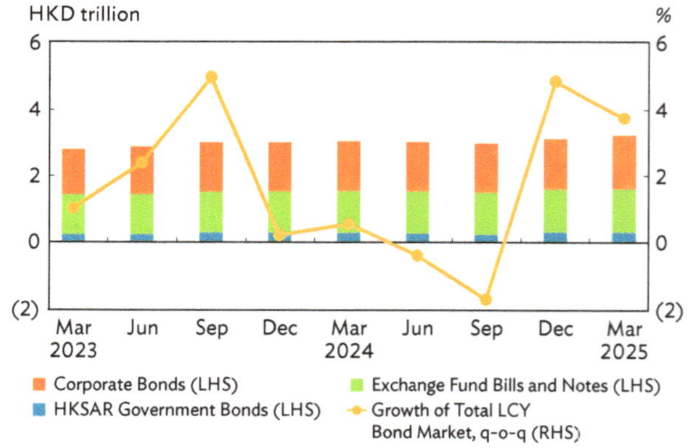

( ) = negative, HKD = Hong Kong dollar, HKSAR = Hong Kong Special Administrative Region, LCY = local currency, LHS = left-hand side, q-o-q = quarter-on-quarter, RHS = right-hand side.

Source: Hong Kong Monetary Authority.

This market summary was written by Debbie Gundaya, consultant, Economic Research and Development Impact Department, Asian Development Bank, Manila.

Total LCY bond sales contracted 0.3% q-o-q in Q1 2025, driven largely by a drop in HKSAR government bond issuance. New issuance of LCY bonds inched down to HKD1,401.7 billion in Q1 2025 from HKD1,406.1 billion in the previous quarter (**Figure 3**). Q1 2025 saw reduced issuance of HKSAR government bonds (HKD7.5 billion) compared to the previous quarter (HKD83.3 billion), when large initial bond sales were launched under the new Infrastructure Bond Programme. Growth in Exchange Fund Bills and Notes issuance also eased to 0.4% q-o-q in Q1 2025 from 0.9% q-o-q in the prior quarter. Meanwhile, growth in corporate debt sales rose to 24.1% q-o-q in Q1 2025 from 17.3% q-o-q in Q4 2024, supported by the fundraising of government-owned corporations such as Airport Authority Hong Kong and Hong Kong Mortgage Corporation. The largest nonbank corporate bank issuer in Q1 2025 was the Airport Authority Hong Kong, which issued HKD18.5 billion of LCY debt (62.7% of total nonbank issuances) as part of a multicurrency bond package intended to fund improvements to its runway system.

Figure 3: Composition of Local Currency Bond Issuance in Hong Kong, China

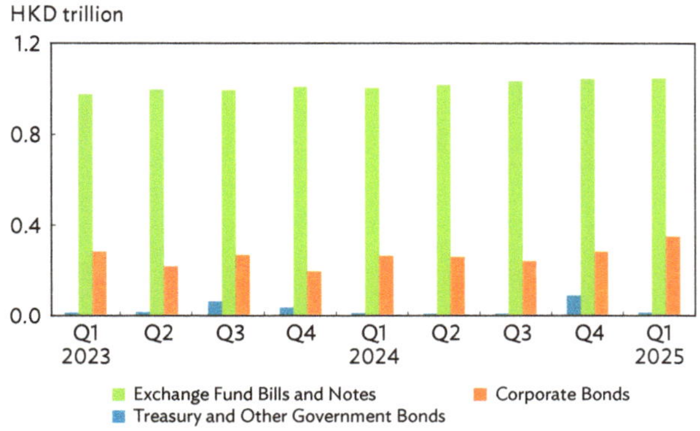

HKD = Hong Kong dollar, Q1 = first quarter, Q2 = second quarter, Q3 = third quarter, Q4 = fourth quarter.

Source: Hong Kong Monetary Authority.

Sustainable Bond Market

Hong Kong, China's stock of sustainable bonds outstanding declined in Q1 2025 due to a contraction in issuance. Sustainable bonds outstanding totaled USD46.6 billion at the end of March, down 3.1% q-o-q as the issuance of new securities contracted amid heightened global uncertainty. Green bonds continued to be the dominant sustainable bond type, comprising 79.0% of the sustainable bond market (**Figure 4**). Government bonds, all of which were green bonds, accounted for 58.2% of the outstanding sustainable bond stock at the end of Q1 2025. Bonds issued by the private sector (41.8% of the total) were primarily green and social bonds. In Q1 2025, new issues of sustainable instruments (USD105.9 million) were green bonds from the private sector. Bonds with tenors of up to 5 years comprised 70.9% of total sustainable bonds outstanding, resulting in a size-weighted average tenor of 4.3 years at the end of March. More than three-quarters of outstanding sustainable bonds in Hong Kong, China were denominated in foreign currencies, among the highest share in emerging East Asia.[10] The United States dollar was the most common denomination of sustainable bonds (43.2% of the total), followed by the Hong Kong dollar (24.1%) and Chinese yuan (20.9%).

Figure 4: Market Profile of Outstanding Sustainable Bonds in Hong Kong, China at the End of March 2025

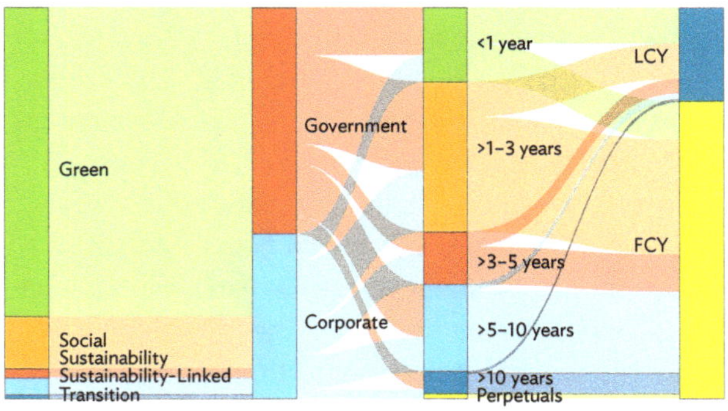

FCY = foreign currency, LCY = local currency.

Source: *AsianBondsOnline* calculations based on Bloomberg LP data.

[10] Emerging East Asia is defined to include member states of the Association of Southeast Asian Nations plus the People's Republic of China; Hong Kong, China; and the Republic of Korea.

Indonesia

Yield Movements

Between 3 March and 30 May, local currency (LCY) government bond yields fell for most maturities in Indonesia as heightened global market uncertainty clouded the economic outlook. Bond yields edged down an average of 16 basis points for maturities of 15 years or less, while they gained an average of 2 basis points for 20 years or more (**Figure 1**). The decline in yields was largely influenced by continued monetary policy easing and a weakening growth outlook. On 20–21 May, Bank Indonesia lowered its policy rate for a second time this year to 5.50% to support economic growth amid a stable domestic currency and low inflation. During its meeting, however, the central bank revised down its 2025 economic growth forecast to 4.6%–5.4% from estimates made in January of 4.7%–5.5%. Real gross domestic product growth ticked down to 4.9% year-on-year in the first quarter (Q1) of 2025 from 5.0% year-on-year in the prior quarter due to a contraction in government expenditures and moderating growth in domestic consumption and fixed investments.

Figure 1: Indonesia's Benchmark Yield Curve—Local Currency Government Bonds

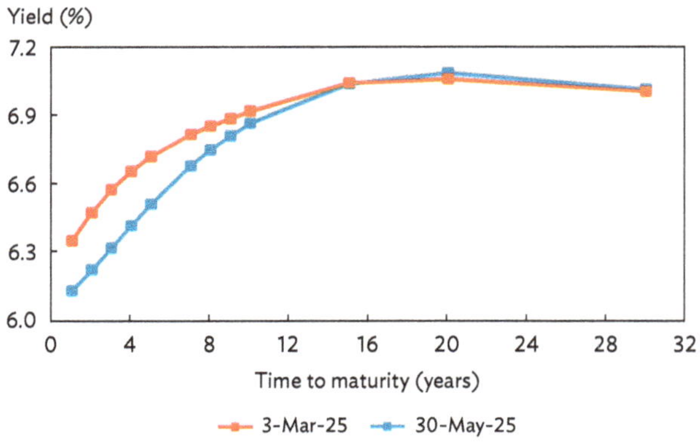

Source: Based on data from Bloomberg LP.

Figure 2: Composition of Local Currency Bonds Outstanding in Indonesia

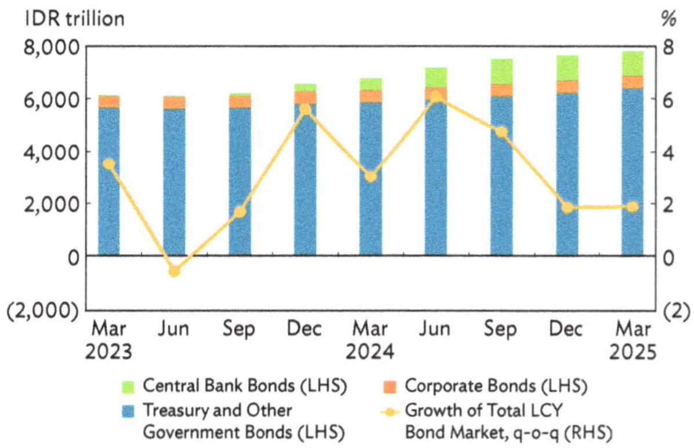

( ) = negative, IDR = Indonesian rupiah, LCY = local currency, LHS = left-hand side, q-o-q = quarter-on-quarter, RHS = right-hand side.

Notes:

1. Data include *sukuk* (Islamic bonds).
2. For end-March 2025, data for treasury and other government bonds are based on *AsianBondsOnline* estimates.

Sources: Bank Indonesia; Directorate General of Budget Financing and Risk Management, Ministry of Finance; and Indonesia Stock Exchange.

Local Currency Bond Market Size and Issuance

Indonesia's LCY bond market reached a size of IDR7,835.3 trillion at the end of March, largely supported by growth in government bonds. The LCY bond market rose 1.9% quarter-on-quarter (q-o-q) in Q1 2025, the same pace as in the fourth quarter (Q4) of 2024. Government bond market growth quickened to 2.7% q-o-q from 2.0% q-o-q, buoyed by increased issuance due to the front-loading strategy of the government (**Figure 2**). As of March, the government said that it had already issued 40.6% of its 2025 debt financing target. Corporate bonds also contributed to the overall growth, albeit to a lesser extent, on moderated growth of 2.2% q-o-q in Q1 2025 from 3.4% q-o-q in the prior quarter. In contrast, central bank securities contracted (–3.4% q-o-q) as maturities exceeded issuance as part of the central bank's move to free up funds for corporate loans.

LCY bond issuance continued to contract in Q1 2025 amid escalating global uncertainties. Total LCY bond issuance tallied IDR638.2 trillion in Q1 2025 on a contraction of 13.2% q-o-q that followed a decline of 5.1% q-o-q in Q4 2024 (**Figure 3**). Issuance of Treasury bonds, however, remained active on growth of 11.8% q-o-q in Q1 2025, reversing the 5.8% q-o-q contraction in the prior quarter, as the government front-loaded its borrowing during the quarter. In contrast, central bank securities shrank 26.4% q-o-q as Bank Indonesia opted to utilize other policy tools for its monetary operations. Corporate bond issuance

This market summary was written by Roselyn Regalado, consultant, Economic Research and Development Impact Department, Asian Development Bank, Manila.

Figure 3: Composition of Local Currency Bond Issuance in Indonesia

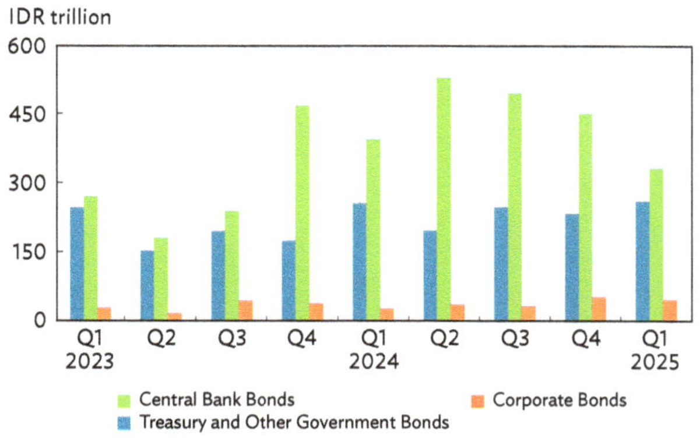

IDR = Indonesian rupiah, Q1 = first quarter, Q2 = second quarter, Q3 = third quarter, Q4 = fourth quarter.

Notes: Data include *sukuk* (Islamic bonds). Data for Treasury and other government bonds comprise tradable and nontradable central government bonds.

Sources: Bank Indonesia; Directorate General of Budget Financing and Risk Management, Ministry of Finance; and Indonesia Stock Exchange.

also declined (–10.5% q-o-q) after gaining 62.2% q-o-q in Q4 2024. During the quarter, corporate bond issuances were led by Tower Bersama Infrastructure and Bank Mandiri, whose respective issuances accounted for 12.0% and 11.0% of the quarterly corporate issuance total.

Investor Profile

At the end of March, the central bank remained the largest holder of Treasury bonds in Indonesia. Around 26.4% of tradable sovereign bonds were held by Bank Indonesia at the end of March, up from its 21.3% holdings share a year earlier. The central bank held 28.9% of all conventional Treasury bonds outstanding, while it held a smaller 15.4% share of *sukuk* (Islamic bonds) (**Figure 4**). The central bank continued to pile up its holdings of Treasury bonds to support its monetary operations.[11] Meanwhile, the holdings shares of all other investor groups have shown marginal change since March 2024, except for banks, which dipped to 18.0% at the end of March 2025 from 24.8% a year earlier.

Figure 4: Investor Profile of Tradable Central Government Bonds

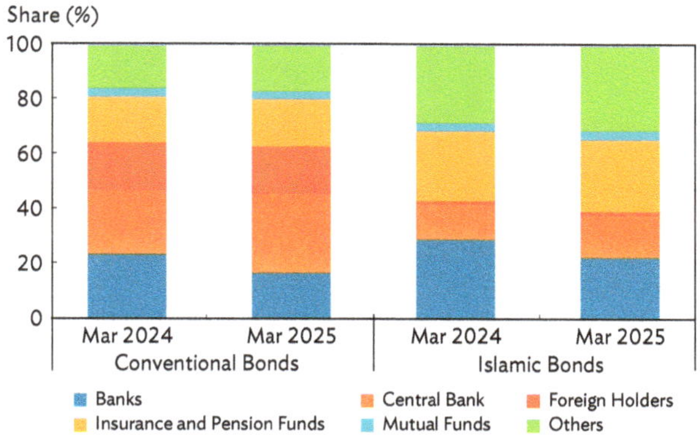

Source: Directorate General of Budget Financing and Risk Management, Ministry of Finance.

Sustainable Bond Market

The sustainable bond market of Indonesia is dominated by green bond instruments, public sector financing, and foreign currency issuances. By the end of March, Indonesia's sustainable bond stock reached USD14.4 billion, expanding by a slower pace of 1.9% q-o-q in Q1 2025 from 3.3% in Q4 2024, dragged down by a contraction in issuance. Green bonds remained the predominant sustainable bond instrument, representing 73.3% of the total, while sustainability bonds accounted for 21.5% (**Figure 5**). About 58.4% of the sustainable bond stock had tenors of over 5 years at the end of March, partly due to the active participation of the government, which accounted for 79.1% of total bonds carrying tenors of more than 5 years. As a result, sustainable bonds in Indonesia had a size-weighted average tenor of 7.7 years at the end of March. Most sustainable bonds outstanding (66.3%) were denominated in a foreign currency—primarily euros, Japanese yen, and US dollars.

Figure 5: Market Profile of Outstanding Sustainable Bonds in Indonesia at the End of March 2025

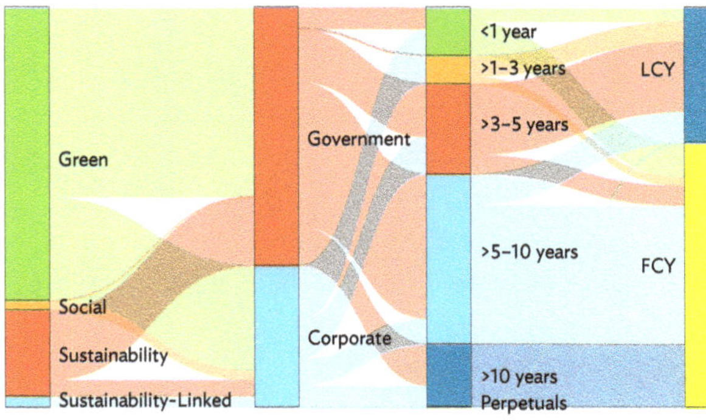

FCY = foreign currency, LCY = local currency.

Source: *AsianBondsOnline* calculations based on Bloomberg LP data.

[11] From 1 January to 20 May, Bank Indonesia purchased an aggregate of about IDR96.4 trillion worth of Treasury bonds, of which about IDR65.0 trillion were purchased from the secondary market and IDR31.4 trillion from the primary market.

Republic of Korea

Yield Movements

Local currency (LCY) government bond yields in the Republic of Korea fell for most maturities between 3 March and 30 May on expectations of further rate cuts by the Bank of Korea (BOK). Yields declined an average of 28 basis points (bps) for maturities between 3 months and 5 years (**Figure 1**). Yields fell on increased expectations of further monetary policy easing by the BOK to support the economy amid stable inflation. The BOK cut the base rate by another 25 bps to 2.50% at its 29 May monetary policy meeting. The BOK previously cut the base rate by 25 bps to 2.75% in February before holding rates steady in April. The BOK also lowered its economic growth forecasts for 2025 and 2026 to 0.8% and 1.6%, respectively, from the February forecasts of 1.5% and 1.8%, as ongoing global trade tensions continue to dampen demand and exports. The Republic of Korea's economy was unchanged in the first quarter (Q1) of 2025, following growth of 1.1% y-o-y in the previous quarter, on slower growth in exports and private and public spending, and a contraction in gross fixed capital formation. Meanwhile, yields for longer-term maturities inched up an average of 9 bps following approval of the first supplementary budget in early May. The government announced plans to increase the proportion of long-term bonds in its adjusted 2025 issuance plan to reflect the supplementary budget, putting upward pressure on yields at the long-end of the curve.

Figure 1: The Republic of Korea's Benchmark Yield Curve—Local Currency Government Bonds

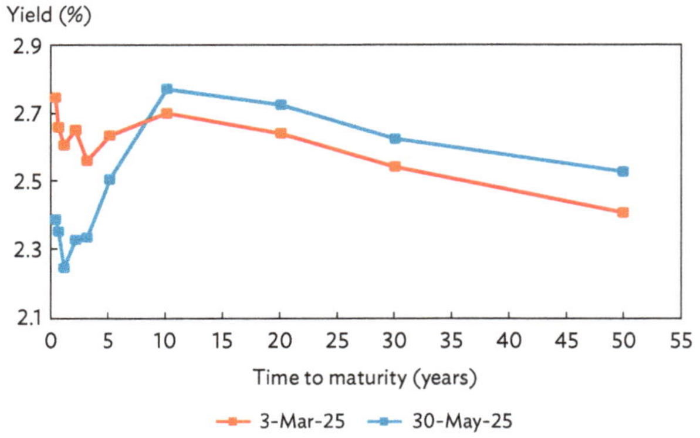

Source: Based on data from Bloomberg LP.

Local Currency Bond Market Size and Issuance

The Republic of Korea's LCY bond market rose at a faster pace in Q1 2025 to reach a size of KRW3,324.6 trillion, solely driven by the government bond segment. Overall growth accelerated to 0.8% quarter-on quarter (q-o-q) from 0.2% q-o-q in the prior quarter. Government bonds outstanding rose 2.6% q-o-q in Q1 2025 due to a surge in issuance during the quarter. Meanwhile, the corporate bond market, which continued to comprise a majority of the total LCY bond market, marginally contracted 0.1% q-o-q in Q1 2025 on reduced issuance (**Figure 2**).

Figure 2: Composition of Local Currency Bonds Outstanding in the Republic of Korea

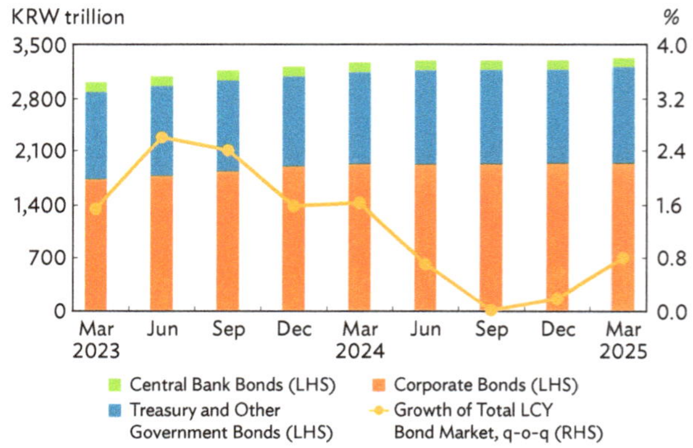

KRW = Korean won, LCY = local currency, LHS = left-hand side, q-o-q = quarter-on-quarter, RHS = right-hand side.
Sources: Bank of Korea and KG Zeroin Corp.

Total LCY bond issuance contracted 12.5% q-o-q to KRW249.4 trillion in Q1 2025, driven by reduced issuance of corporate bonds. Sales of corporate bonds fell 31.0% q-o-q in Q1 2025 amid the weak economic outlook brought about by global trade tensions (**Figure 3**). Meanwhile, the issuance of government bonds surged 79.5% q-o-q in Q1 2025 to support the government's front-loading policy of spending 75% of the total budget in the first half of the year.

This market summary was written by Angelica Andrea Cruz, consultant, Economic Research and Development Impact Department, Asian Development Bank, Manila.

Figure 3: Composition of Local Currency Bond Issuance in the Republic of Korea

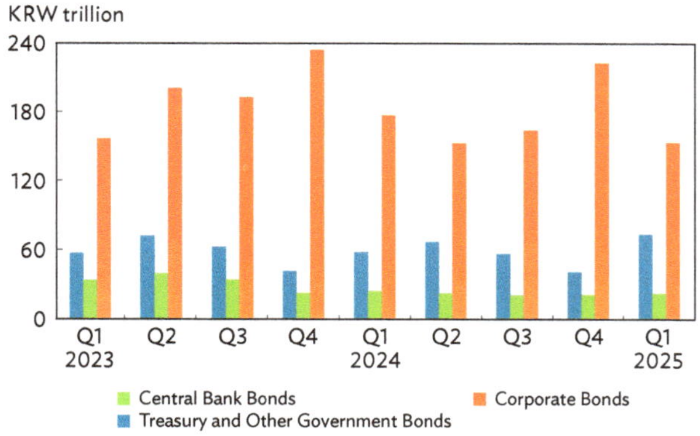

KRW = Korean won, Q1 = first quarter, Q2 = second quarter, Q3 = third quarter, Q4 = fourth quarter.

Sources: Bank of Korea and KG Zeroin Corp.

Investor Profile

The Republic of Korea's LCY government bond market continued to have one of the most diverse investor bases in emerging East Asia in 2024.[12] The government bond market's investor profile was barely changed at the end of December from a year earlier, with the stock of outstanding bonds continuing to be held by five major investor groups (**Figure 4**). Insurance companies and pension funds remained the largest investor group in the government bond market with a share of 30.4%, followed by foreign investors (19.8%) and banks (19.6%). Meanwhile, the Republic of Korea's LCY corporate bond market is still dominated by two major investor groups who together held a collective share of 72.2% at the end of 2024: other financial institutions held 43.5% of the corporate bond market, followed by insurance companies and pension funds with a share of 28.7%. Foreign holdings in the corporate bond market remained negligible.

Figure 4: Local Currency Bonds Outstanding Investor Profile

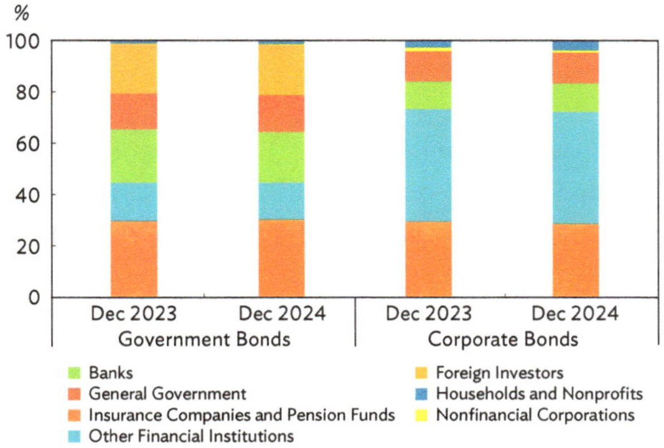

Sources: *AsianBondsOnline* and Bank of Korea.

Sustainable Bond Market

Firms from the public and private sectors continued to be active issuers in the Republic of Korea's sustainable bond market. The Republic of Korea's sustainable bond market contracted slightly by 0.6% q-o-q to reach a size of USD183.1 billion at the end of Q1 2025. Sustainable bonds outstanding issued by private companies comprised 52.6% of the total, while the public sector accounted for the remaining 47.4% (**Figure 5**). By bond type, social bonds—almost three-quarters of which come from the public sector—dominate the Republic of Korea's total sustainable bond market with a share of 54.0%. Green bonds followed with a 28.2% share, mostly issued by the private sector. Nearly 70% of sustainable bonds outstanding at the end of March had remaining tenors of 3 years or less, resulting in a size-weighted average tenor of 3 years. The Korean won continued to be the predominant currency of outstanding sustainable bonds with a share of 58.8%. This was followed by the United States dollar (29.8%) and the euro (8.0%).

Figure 5: Market Profile of Outstanding Sustainable Bonds in the Republic of Korea at the End of March 2025

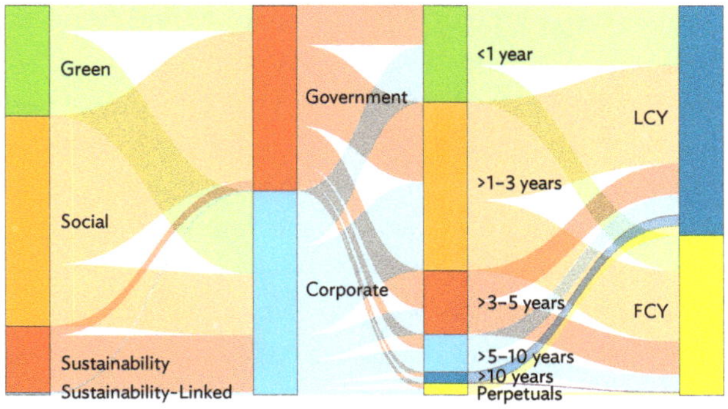

FCY = foreign currency, LCY = local currency.

Source: *AsianBondsOnline* calculations based on Bloomberg LP data.

[12] Emerging East Asia is defined to include member states of the Association of Southeast Asian Nations plus the People's Republic of China; Hong Kong, China; and the Republic of Korea.

Malaysia

Yield Movements

Malaysia's local currency (LCY) government bond yield curve shifted downward between 3 March and 30 May. Bond yields fell an average of 26 basis points across all maturities amid a weakening outlook for domestic growth and escalating global economic uncertainties (**Figure 1**). On 8 May, Bank Negara Malaysia kept the overnight policy rate at 3.00%, with the possibility of a reduction if necessary, noting that downside risks to economic growth have increased due to sharper-than-expected economic slowdowns among key trading partners, heightened uncertainties impacting consumption and investment, and lower-than-anticipated commodity production. Further, Bank Negara Malaysia reduced the statutory reserve requirement ratio from 2.0% to 1.0% to spur financial market activities. The central bank also hinted at a potential downward revision to Malaysia's 2025 growth projection, which currently stands at 4.5%–5.5%. In the first quarter (Q1) of 2025, the Malaysian economy grew 4.4% year-on-year, slower than the previous quarter's 4.9% year-on-year, weighed down by moderating growth in private consumption, exports, and imports. Additionally, domestic growth was dampened amid a contraction in the mining and quarrying sector.

Figure 1: Malaysia's Benchmark Yield Curve—Local Currency Government Bonds

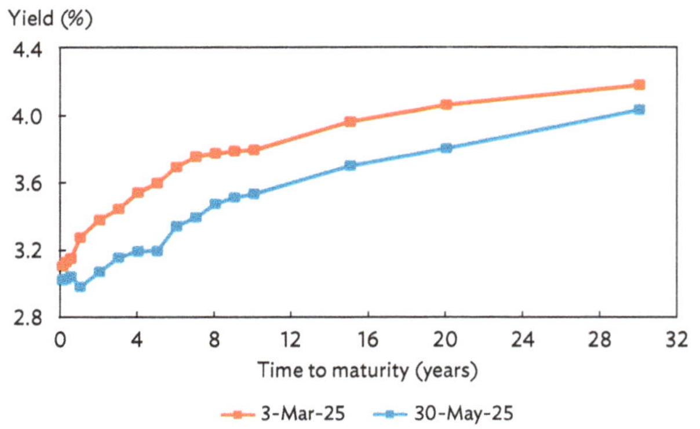

Source: Based on data from Bloomberg LP.

Figure 2: Composition of Local Currency Bonds Outstanding in Malaysia

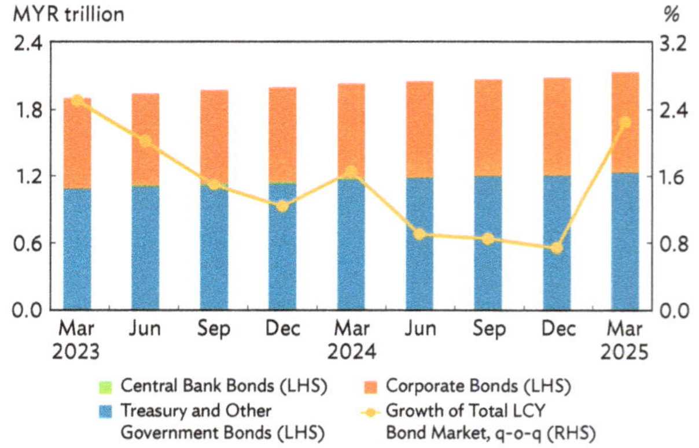

LCY = local currency, LHS = left-hand side, MYR = Malaysian ringgit, q-o-q = quarter-on-quarter, RHS = right-hand side.

Source: Bank Negara Malaysia Fully Automated System for Issuing/Tendering.

Local Currency Bond Market Size and Issuance

The LCY bond market of Malaysia expanded in Q1 2025 to reach a size of MYR2.1 trillion at the end of March, driven by faster growth in both Treasuries and corporate bonds. The LCY bond market exhibited growth of 2.3% quarter-on-quarter (q-o-q) in Q1 2025, a faster pace than the previous quarter's 0.8% (**Figure 2**). Outstanding Treasuries and other government bonds increased 2.4% q-o-q, versus 0.6% q-o-q in the quarter prior, due to a higher volume of issuance. Malaysia's corporate bond segment posted 2.0% q-o-q growth in Q1 2025 despite a contraction in issuance due to a lower volume of maturities during the quarter. The central bank has not issued new securities since the third quarter of 2024, resulting in zero outstanding central bank bills at the end of March. *Sukuk* (Islamic bonds) dominated the LCY bond market at the end of March, comprising 63.6% of total bonds outstanding.

Led by government bonds, LCY bond issuance expanded 23.9% q-o-q to MYR99.6 billion in Q1 2025. Government bond issuance rose 63.5% q-o-q, reversing the previous quarter's 43.4% q-o-q contraction, following increases in bond sales of both conventional bonds and *sukuk* (**Figure 3**). On the other hand, corporate bond issuance contracted 1.6% q-o-q in Q1 2025. The largest issuer of LCY corporate bonds in Q1 2025 was Cagamas, having issued MYR5.7 billion worth of conventional and *sukuk* commercial paper and Islamic medium-term-notes, accounting for 11.8% of total LCY corporate issuance during the quarter.

This market summary was written by Justin Adrian Villas, consultant, Economic Research and Development Impact Department, Asian Development Bank, Manila.

Figure 3: Composition of Local Currency Bond Issuance in Malaysia

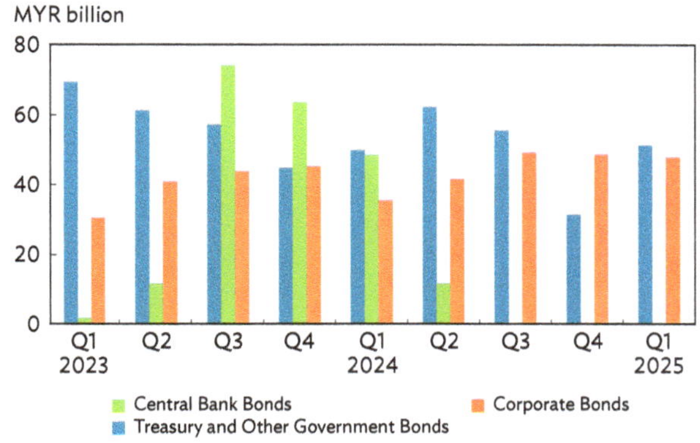

MYR = Malaysian ringgit, Q1 = first quarter, Q2 = second quarter, Q3 = third quarter, Q4 = fourth quarter.

Source: Bank Negara Malaysia Fully Automated System for Issuing/Tendering.

Investor Profile

At the end of December, domestic investors held 78.7% of Malaysia's LCY government bonds outstanding. The two largest holdings shares belonged to financial institutions and social security institutions at 31.5% and 30.7%, respectively (**Figure 4**). Foreign holdings in Malaysia's government bond market edged down to 21.3% at the end of December 2024, compared to 22.5% a year prior, due partly to uncertainties over the future path of monetary policy in the United States. Nonetheless, Malaysia's foreign holdings share remained the highest among its emerging East Asian peers.[13]

Figure 4: Local Currency Government Bonds Investor Profile

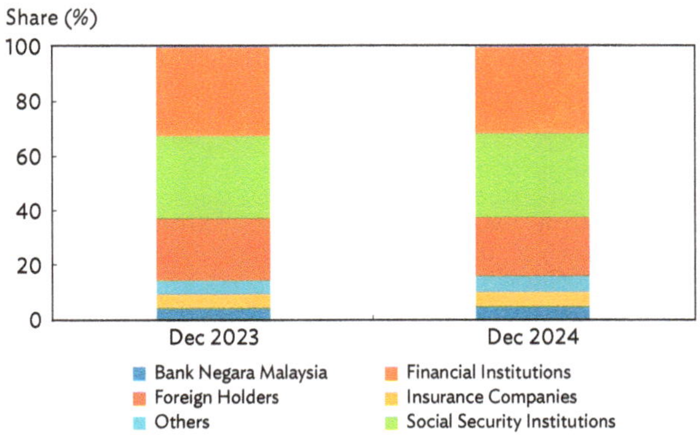

Note: "Others" include statutory bodies, nominees and trustee companies, and cooperatives and unclassified items.

Source: Bank Negara Malaysia.

Sustainable Bond Market

Sustainable bonds outstanding in Malaysia at the end of March mostly comprised sustainability bonds, corporate issuances, and bonds denominated in Malaysian ringgit. Total sustainable bonds outstanding tallied USD15.7 billion at the end of March on growth of 1.9% q-o-q, with most issuances denominated in Malaysian ringgit (88.2%). By type of bond, sustainability bonds comprised a majority of the sustainable bond stock (70.2%), followed by green bonds (19.2%) (**Figure 5**). Malaysia's sustainable bond market is dominated by corporate bonds, which comprised 77.6% of total outstanding sustainable bonds at the end of March. Further, 59.8% of corporate sustainable bonds outstanding carried tenors of more than 5 years. Bonds issued by the public sector comprised 22.4% of outstanding sustainable bonds, all of which carried tenors of more than 5 years. At the end of March, the size-weighted average tenor in Malaysia's sustainable bond market was 8.6 years.

Figure 5: Market Profile of Outstanding Sustainable Bonds in Malaysia at the End of March 2025

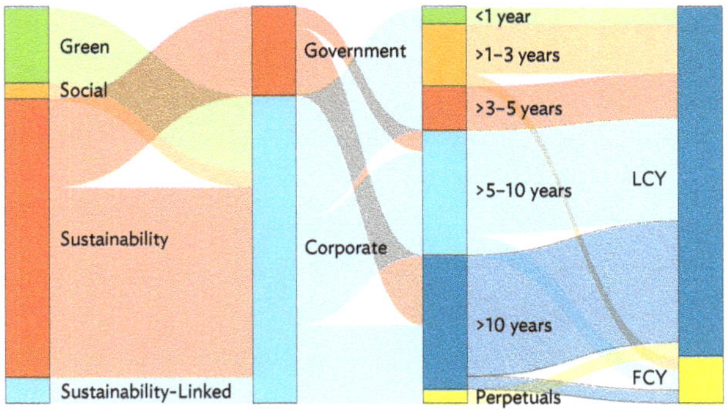

FCY = foreign currency, LCY = local currency.

Source: *AsianBondsOnline* calculations based on Bloomberg LP data.

[13] Emerging East Asia is defined to include member states of the Association of Southeast Asian Nations plus the People's Republic of China; Hong Kong, China; and the Republic of Korea.

Philippines

Yield Movements

Local currency (LCY) government bond yield movements in the Philippines were mixed between 3 March and 30 May. Yields at the short-end (1–3 months) and long-end (7 years and longer) of the curve rose an average of 17 basis points (bps), largely tracking the yield movements of United States Treasuries (**Figure 1**). In contrast, yields for maturities of 6 months to 5 years fell an average of 7 bps, driven by the Bangko Sentral ng Pilipinas' (BSP) 25 bps rate cut on 10 April. The BSP lowered its overnight reverse repurchase rate to 5.50% amid slowing inflation and elevated risks to growth due to a challenging external environment. Year-on-year inflation eased further to 1.3% in May from 1.4% in April and 1.8% in March, due to slower increases in food and utility prices. The decline in yields was also influenced by the BSP's shift toward a more accommodative monetary policy stance to support growth amid external challenges, fueling market expectations of more rate cuts this year.

Figure 1: The Philippines' Benchmark Yield Curve—Local Currency Government Bonds

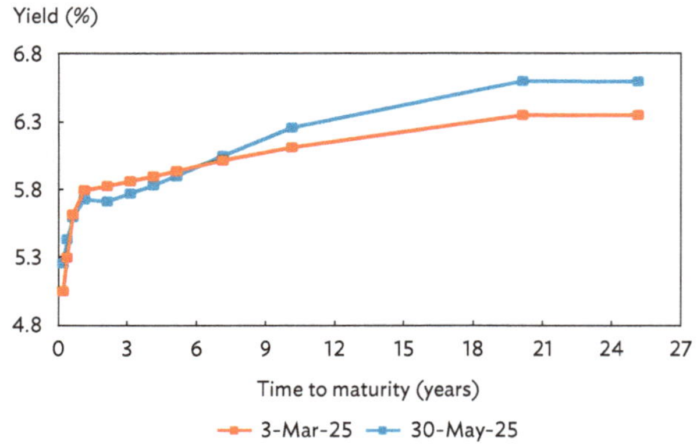

Source: Based on data from Bloomberg LP.

Local Currency Bond Market Size and Issuance

Growth in the LCY bond market rebounded in the first quarter (Q1) of 2025, supported by robust expansions of government bonds and central bank securities. The stock of LCY bonds reached PHP13.5 trillion at the end of March, expanding 4.1% quarter-on-quarter (q-o-q) following the previous quarter's 0.6% q-o-q contraction (**Figure 2**). Growth was steered by a rebound in Treasury and other government bonds, which rose 4.1% q-o-q due to increased government borrowing. Meanwhile, central bank securities posted the fastest rate of expansion among all bond types at 15.3% q-o-q, reversing the 11.7% q-o-q contraction in the previous quarter. Conversely, despite an increase in issuance, the corporate debt stock contracted 2.8% q-o-q in Q1 2025 due to a high volume of maturities.

Figure 2: Composition of Local Currency Bonds Outstanding in the Philippines

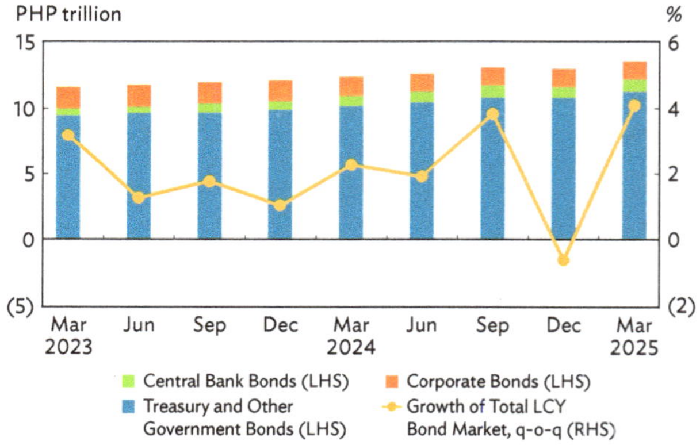

( ) = negative, LCY = local currency, LHS = left-hand side, PHP = Philippine peso, q-o-q = quarter-on-quarter, RHS = right-hand side.

Note: Treasury and other government bonds comprise Treasury bonds, Treasury bills, and bonds issued by government agencies, entities, and corporations for which repayment is guaranteed by the Government of the Philippines.

Sources: Bangko Sentral ng Pilipinas, Bureau of the Treasury, and Bloomberg LP.

LCY bond issuance recovered in Q1 2025, fueled by increased issuance in both the government and corporate sectors. Overall issuance growth jumped 13.7% q-o-q to a total of PHP2.7 trillion in Q1 2025 (**Figure 3**). Growth was largely driven by government bond issuance, which surged 98.8% q-o-q as the government front-loaded its borrowing for the year. Similarly, corporate bond issuance grew 20.6% q-o-q in Q1 2025 after declining 63.3% q-o-q in the previous quarter, as corporate issuers sought funds to refinance their maturing debt. SM Prime Holdings was the largest corporate bond issuer during the quarter, with total debt sale of PHP25.0 billion, or 34.2% of the corporate issuance total.

This market summary was written by Jeremy Grace Ilustrisimo, consultant, Economic Research and Development Impact Department, Asian Development Bank, Manila.

Figure 3: Composition of Local Currency Bond Issuance in the Philippines

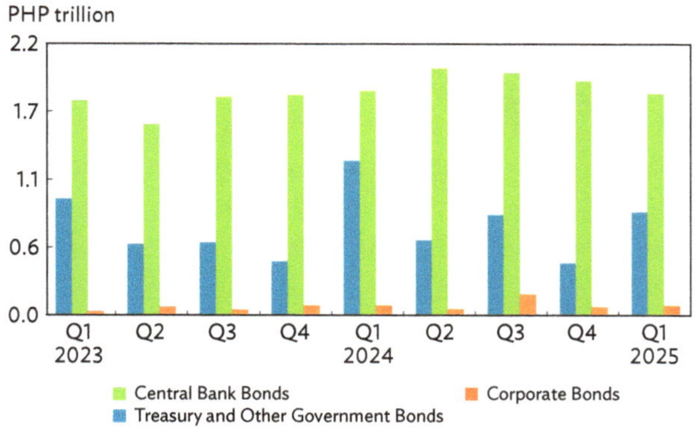

PHP = Philippine peso, Q1 = first quarter, Q2 = second quarter, Q3 = third quarter, Q4 = fourth quarter.

Note: Treasury and other government bonds comprise Treasury bonds, Treasury bills, and bonds issued by government agencies, entities, and corporations for which repayment is guaranteed by the Government of the Philippines.

Sources: Bangko Sentral ng Pilipinas, Bureau of the Treasury, and Bloomberg LP.

Figure 4: Investor Profile of Local Currency Government Bonds

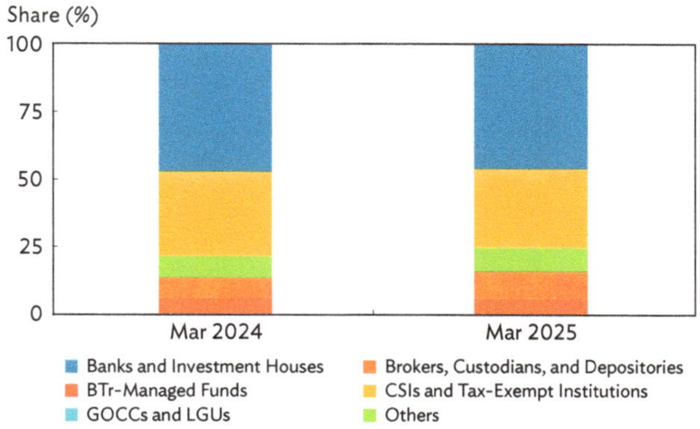

BTr = Bureau of the Treasury, CSI = contractual savings institution, GOCC = government-owned or -controlled corporation, LGU = local government unit.

Note: At the end of March, the aggregate holdings share for government-owned or -controlled corporations and local government units was 0.003%, amounting to PHP0.3 billion.

Source: Bureau of the Treasury.

Investor Profile

The investor structure of the Philippines' LCY government bond market remained dominated by two investor groups. These two dominant groups—(i) banks and investment houses, and (ii) contractual savings institutions and tax-exempt institutions—collectively held about 75.0% of the LCY government debt stock at the end of March, down from 78.3% a year earlier (**Figure 4**). Meanwhile, the share of bonds held by brokers, custodians, and depositories rose to 10.4% during the same period, up from 7.8% the previous year, making them the third-largest investor group at the end of March.

Sustainable Bond Market

Sustainability instruments continued to dominate the Philippines' sustainable bond market in Q1 2025. Sustainability bonds accounted for 86.5% of the market's total sustainable debt stock in Q1 2025, followed by green bonds and sustainability-linked bonds with market shares of 11.7% and 1.8%, respectively (**Figure 5**). During Q1 2025, total outstanding sustainable bonds grew 20.6% q-o-q to reach USD13.6 billion at the end of March. The Philippines' sustainable bond market is among the smallest in emerging East Asia, comprising only 2.0% of the region's total.[14] Nearly 55.0% of the market's total sustainable debt stock has been issued by the public sector, while over 70.0% is denominated in a foreign currency. Bonds carrying tenors of over 10 years comprised 48.8% of the total sustainable debt stock at the end of March, resulting in a size-weighted average tenor of 12.6 years. In February, the Philippines issued a EUR-denominated sustainability bond worth USD1.0 billion, marking the government's first EUR-denominated sustainability bond.

Figure 5: Market Profile of Outstanding Sustainable Bonds in the Philippines at the End of March 2025

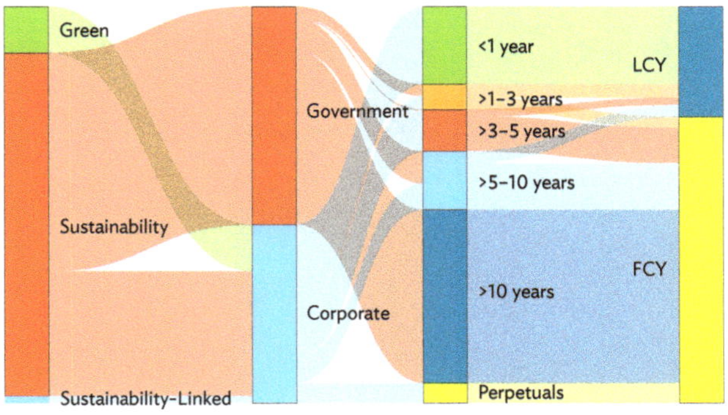

FCY = foreign currency, LCY = local currency.

Source: *AsianBondsOnline* calculations based on Bloomberg LP data.

[14] Emerging East Asia is defined to include member states of the Association of Southeast Asian Nations plus the People's Republic of China; Hong Kong, China; and the Republic of Korea.

Singapore

Yield Movements

Between 3 March and 30 May, local currency (LCY) government bond yields in Singapore fell for all maturities. During the review period, yields fell an average of 45 basis points across the curve, largely driven by the Monetary Authority of Singapore's (MAS) monetary policy easing and the weakened economic growth outlook (**Figure 1**). On 14 April, MAS reduced the slope of the Singapore dollar's nominal effective exchange rate, while retaining its width and the level at which it is centered, for a second time this year due to slowing economic growth and moderating inflation expectations. In the first quarter (Q1) of 2025, Singapore's economy expanded 3.9% year-on-year (y-o-y), down from the previous quarter's growth of 5.0% y-o-y amid cooling in the manufacturing and trade-related services sectors. Additionally, MAS reduced its inflation forecast for 2025 to 0.5%–1.5% from its January estimate of 1.5%–2.5%. In April, consumer price inflation remained at 0.9% y-o-y, the same as in February and March, and down from January's 1.2% y-o-y.

Figure 1: Singapore's Benchmark Yield Curve—Local Currency Government Bonds

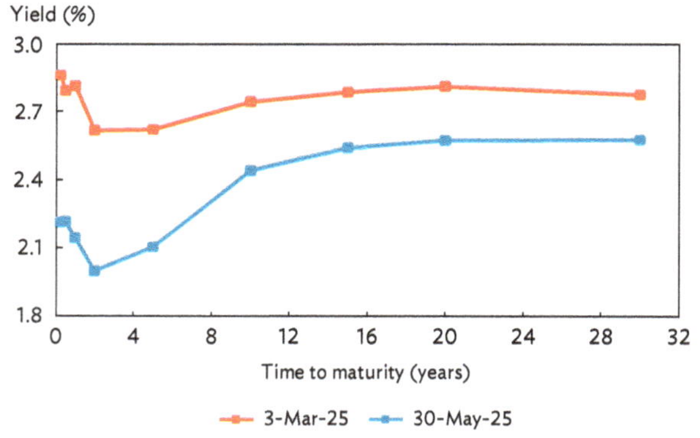

Source: Based on data from Bloomberg LP.

Local Currency Bond Market Size and Issuance

Singapore's LCY bond market expanded to a size of SGD866.9 billion at the end of March, buoyed by growth in outstanding MAS bills. The LCY bond stock in Q1 2025 grew 2.0% quarter-on-quarter (q-o-q), faster than the fourth quarter (Q4) of 2024's growth of 1.6% q-o-q (**Figure 2**). MAS bills outstanding grew at a pace of 1.5% q-o-q, up from the prior quarter's 1.2% q-o-q. The Treasuries and other government bonds segment also saw accelerated expansion during the quarter, growing 3.5% q-o-q versus the previous quarter's 1.4% q-o-q, on reduced maturities. On the other hand, corporate bonds outstanding only expanded 0.7% q-o-q in Q1 2025, much slower than Q4 2024's 2.5% q-o-q growth.

Figure 2: Composition of Local Currency Bonds Outstanding in Singapore

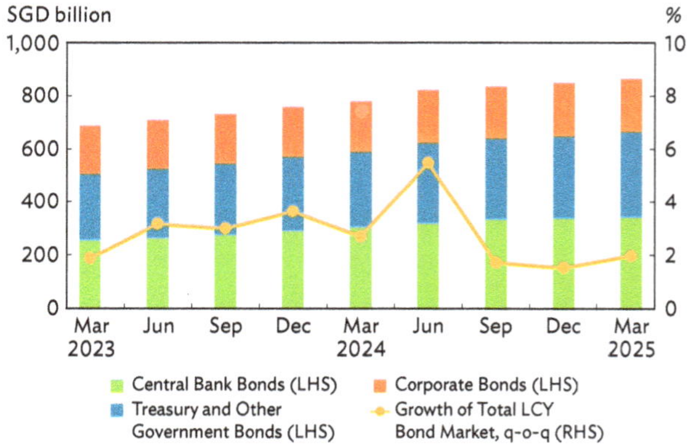

LCY = local currency, LHS = left-hand side, q-o-q = quarter-on-quarter, RHS = right-hand side, SGD = Singapore dollar.

Note: Corporate bonds are based on *AsianBondsOnline* estimates.

Sources: Monetary Authority of Singapore and Bloomberg LP.

This market summary was written by Justin Adrian Villas, consultant, Economic Research and Development Impact Department, Asian Development Bank, Manila.

Total LCY bond issuance declined in Q1 2025, with growth moderating across all bond segments. Total issuance grew 0.7% q-o-q, lagging behind the previous quarter's pace of 3.0% q-o-q (**Figure 3**). Issuance of MAS bills and Treasuries and other government bonds in Q1 2025 only saw q-o-q growth of 0.8% and 0.2%, respectively, down from expansions of 2.7% and 3.6% in Q4 2024. The corporate bond segment saw a contraction in issuance of 2.0%, reversing the prior quarter's growth of 30.4% q-o-q, amid dampened business confidence and the uncertain external economic outlook. The Housing & Development Board was the largest corporate bond issuer during the quarter having issued fixed-rate notes amounting to SGD1.7 billion, accounting for 36.0% of total corporate issuance.

Figure 3: Composition of Local Currency Bond Issuance in Singapore

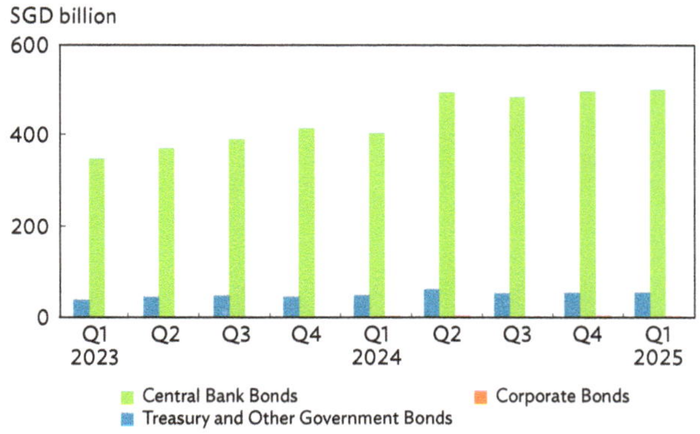

Q1 = first quarter, Q2 = second quarter, Q3 = third quarter, Q4 = fourth quarter, SGD = Singapore dollar.

Note: Corporate bonds are based on *AsianBondsOnline* estimates.

Sources: Monetary Authority of Singapore and Bloomberg LP.

Sustainable Bond Market

Green bond instruments continued to dominate Singapore's sustainable bond market, accounting for 83.8% of the total sustainable bond stock at the end of March. Sustainable bonds outstanding rose to USD26.6 billion at the end of Q1 2025, posting growth of 2.3% q-o-q (**Figure 4**). Most sustainable bonds (82.4%) were LCY-denominated. Bonds carrying tenors of over 5 years comprised 59.7% of total outstanding sustainable bonds at the end of March, resulting in a size-weighted average tenor of 16.2 years for sustainable bonds in Singapore, the longest average tenor among all emerging East Asian sustainable bond markets.[15] The state-owned Housing & Development Board was Singapore's largest issuer of sustainable bonds during the quarter, issuing 5-year green bonds in January totaling SGD950.0 million, which accounted for 74.0% of total sustainable bond quarterly issuance, in fulfillment of its Green Finance Framework.

Figure 4: Market Profile of Outstanding Sustainable Bonds in Singapore at the End of March 2025

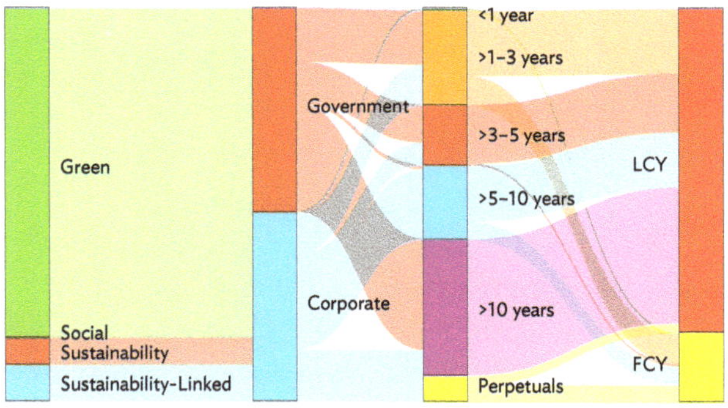

FCY = foreign currency, LCY = local currency.

Source: *AsianBondsOnline* calculations based on Bloomberg LP data.

[15] Emerging East Asia is defined to include member states of the Association of Southeast Asian Nations plus the People's Republic of China; Hong Kong, China; and the Republic of Korea.

Thailand

Yield Movements

Between 3 March and 30 May, Thailand's local currency (LCY) government bond yields fell for all maturities amid monetary policy easing by the Bank of Thailand (BOT). Yields declined an average of 34 basis points across all maturities (**Figure 1**). The downtrend in yields was largely influenced by the BOT's continued monetary policy loosening to address downside risks to economic growth. The BOT reduced its policy rate by 25 basis points to 1.75% on 30 April, noting that the growth outlook faced further risks from global trade tensions. The central bank lowered its gross domestic product growth forecast for full-year 2025 to 1.3% (if trade negotiations with the United States result in lower tariffs) or 2.0% (if negotiations result in higher tariffs) from its December projection of 2.9%. Thailand's economy expanded 3.1% year-on-year in the first quarter (Q1) of 2025, down from 3.3% year-on-year in the previous quarter on slower growth in government and private consumption, and a contraction in private investment.

Figure 1: Thailand's Benchmark Yield Curve—Local Currency Government Bonds

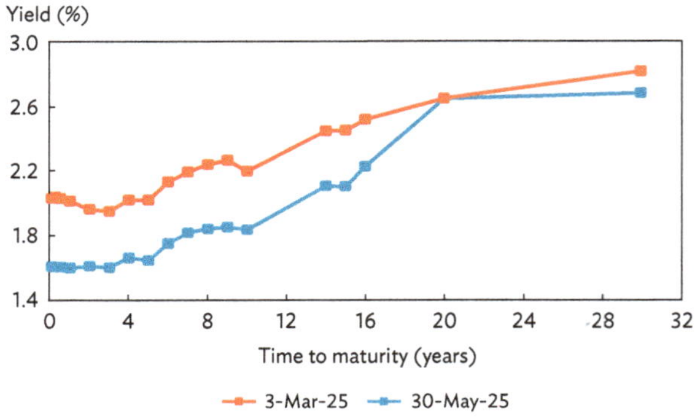

Sources: Based on data from Bloomberg LP and Thai Bond Market Association.

Figure 2: Composition of Local Currency Bonds Outstanding in Thailand

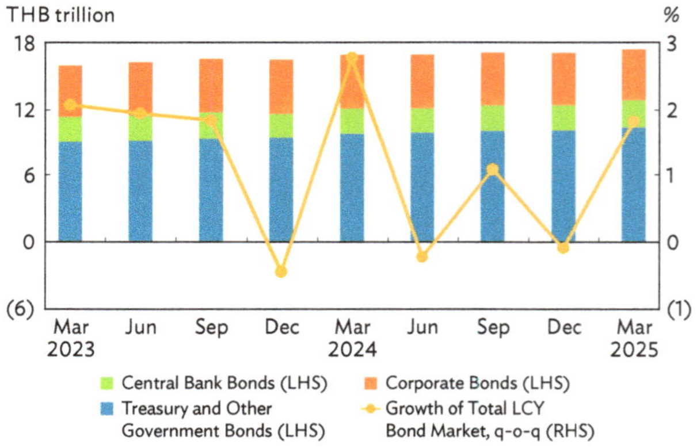

( ) = negative, LCY = local currency, LHS = left-hand side, q-o-q = quarter-on-quarter, RHS = right-hand side, THB = Thai baht.

Sources: Bank of Thailand and Thai Bond Market Association.

Local Currency Bond Market Size and Issuance

Thailand's LCY bonds outstanding rebounded in Q1 2025. The LCY bond market reached a size of THB17.4 trillion at the end of March, growing 1.8% quarter-on-quarter (q-o-q) in Q1 2025 after a nominal 0.1% q-o-q contraction in the fourth quarter (Q4) of 2024 (**Figure 2**). Growth in outstanding government bonds (THB10.4 trillion) quickened to 2.6% q-o-q in Q1 2025 from 0.8% q-o-q in Q4 2024, due to a smaller volume of maturities and a modest rise in issuance. BOT bonds outstanding (THB2.5 trillion) rebounded, rising 6.0% q-o-q in Q1 2025 after falling 0.8% q-o-q in the prior quarter due to increased issuance. Meanwhile, the LCY corporate bond stock (THB4.5 trillion) declined further, contracting 2.0% q-o-q in Q1 2025 after falling 1.6% q-o-q in Q4 2024, dragged down by declining issuance amid weak investor sentiment.

LCY bond sales rebounded in Q1 2025, supported by increased issuance of government and BOT bonds. Issuance of LCY bonds grew 2.4% q-o-q to THB2.1 trillion in Q1 2025, reversing a 5.7% q-o-q contraction in the previous quarter (**Figure 3**). Treasury and other government bond issuance (THB0.6 trillion) posted modest growth of 0.2% q-o-q in Q1 2025 versus a 9.4% q-o-q fall in the prior quarter, driven by increased issuance of Treasury bills and state-owned enterprise bonds. BOT issuance (THB1.2 trillion) also rebounded, rising 5.0% q-o-q in Q1 2025 versus a 1.0% q-o-q contraction in Q4 2024, mainly due to increased issuance of short-term securities in response to market

This market summary was written by Debbie Gundaya, consultant, Economic Research and Development Impact Department, Asian Development Bank, Manila.

Figure 3: Composition of Local Currency Bond Issuance in Thailand

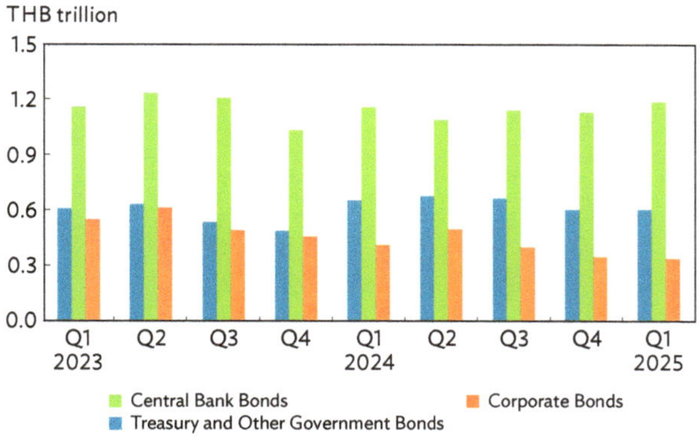

Q1 = first quarter, Q2 = second quarter, Q3 = third quarter, Q4 = fourth quarter, THB = Thai baht.

Sources: Bank of Thailand and Thai Bond Market Association.

Figure 4: Investor Profile of Government Bonds in Thailand

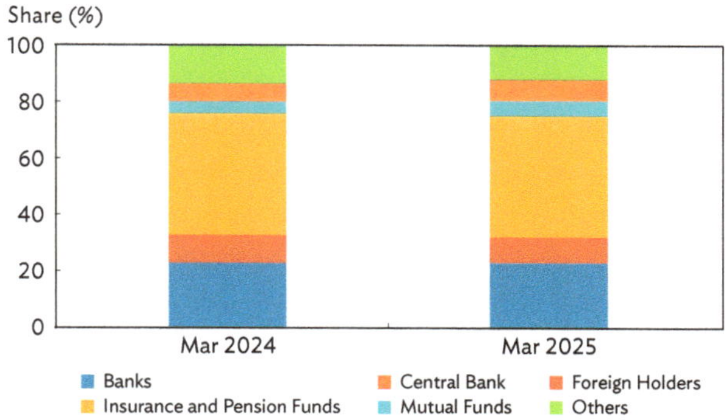

Source: Bank of Thailand.

conditions. Meanwhile, corporate bond sales continued to contract, falling 2.5% q-o-q in Q1 2025 amid heightened uncertainty over the economic outlook. Gulf Energy Development was the largest corporate bond issuer in Q1 2025 with aggregate issuance of THB30.0 billion, which accounted for 8.9% of total corporate debt sales.

Investor Profile

Institutional investors remained the primary holders of Thai LCY government bonds. The combined holdings of insurance and pension funds, banks, and mutual funds rose slightly to 71.6% at the end of March 2025 from 70.4% a year earlier (**Figure 4**). BOT holdings rose to 7.6% from 6.4% during the same period as the central bank purchased a total of THB92.3 billion of government securities in line with monetary operations.

Sustainable Bond Market

Thailand's sustainable bond market largely comprised sustainability instruments issued by the public sector and denominated in local currency. Thailand's sustainable bond market rose 1.0% q-o-q to USD24.3 billion at the end of March. Sustainability instruments (USD15.7 billion) were the predominant bond type, comprising 64.8% of the total (**Figure 5**). Green bonds (USD4.4 billion) followed, accounting for 18.2% of outstanding sustainable bonds. About 66.7% of all outstanding sustainable bonds were issued by the public sector. Government-issued bonds were largely sustainability instruments, while corporate-issued instruments were dominated by green bonds. Over 60% of outstanding sustainable bonds had a remaining tenor longer than 10 years, resulting in a size-weighted average tenor of 8.6 years at the end of March. About 98.4% of Thai sustainable bonds were LCY-denominated, which remained among the highest shares in emerging East Asian markets.[16]

Figure 5: Market Profile of Outstanding Sustainable Bonds in Thailand at the End of March 2025

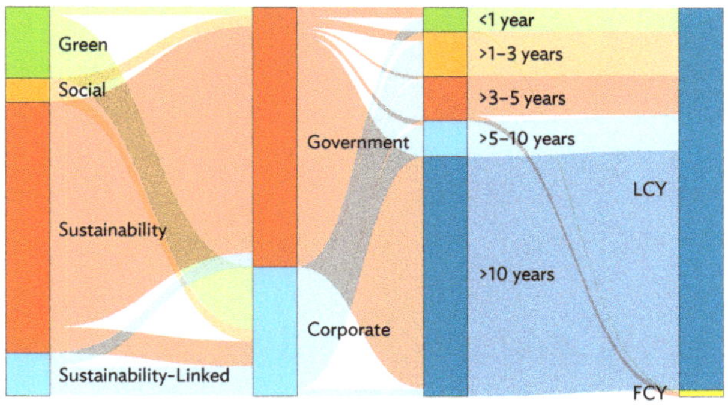

FCY = foreign currency, LCY = local currency.

Source: *AsianBondsOnline* calculations based on Bloomberg LP data.

[16] Emerging East Asia is defined to include member states of the Association of Southeast Asian Nations plus the People's Republic of China; Hong Kong, China; and the Republic of Korea.

Viet Nam

Yield Movements

Between 3 March and 30 May, the local currency (LCY) government bond yield curve in Viet Nam was relatively steady. Yields across the curve moved an average of 3 basis points amid market expectations that the State Bank of Vietnam will keep its refinancing rate unchanged, at least through the first half of 2025, to foster economic growth (**Figure 1**). The central bank has held the policy rate steady at 4.50% since June 2023. On 6 April, the government maintained its full-year 2025 growth target of at least 8.0% despite global trade uncertainties, following 7.1% growth in 2024. Viet Nam's economy grew 6.9% year-on-year (y-o-y) in the first quarter (Q1) of 2025, which was slower than the 7.6% y-o-y growth recorded in the previous quarter due to softened growth in both the service (7.7% y-o-y), and industry and construction (7.4% y-o-y) sectors amid a slowdown in global demand. Despite a slight uptick, inflation remained within the government's ceiling of 4.5%. In May, y-o-y inflation inched-up to 3.2% from 3.1% in April and March, driven by increases in electricity and housing prices.

Figure 1: Viet Nam's Benchmark Yield Curve—Local Currency Government Bonds

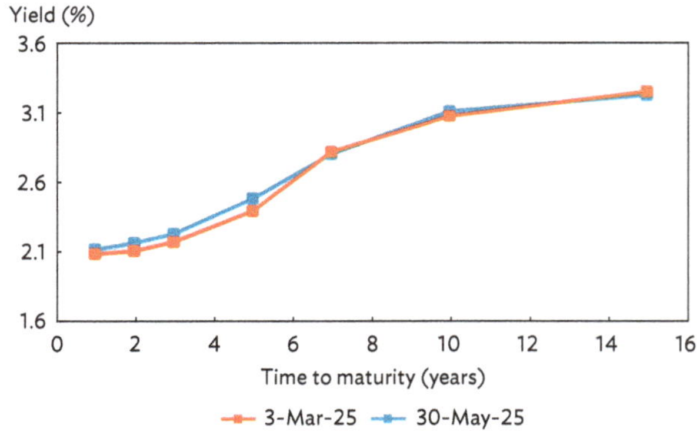

Source: Based on data from Bloomberg LP.

Local Currency Bond Market Size and Issuance

LCY bond market growth slowed in Q1 2025, dragged down by a contraction in central bank securities. At the end of March, total LCY bonds outstanding reached VND3,222.5 trillion, posting moderated quarter-on-quarter (q-o-q) growth of 1.9%, down from 5.0% in the previous quarter (**Figure 2**). The slowdown was largely driven by a contraction in the stock of central bank securities (–32.1% q-o-q) due to a large volume of maturities. Additionally, because of the low volume of issuance during the quarter, the total corporate debt stock also posted slower growth of 1.0% q-o-q in Q1 2025 versus 4.4% q-o-q in the previous quarter. Meanwhile, Treasury and other government bonds grew 4.4% q-o-q at the end of March amid increased government borrowing.

Figure 2: Composition of Local Currency Bonds Outstanding in Viet Nam

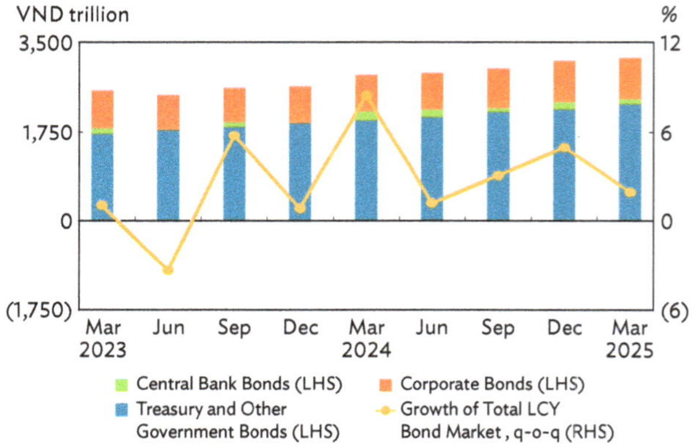

( ) = negative, LCY = local currency, LHS = left-hand side, q-o-q = quarter-on-quarter, RHS = right-hand side, VND = Vietnamese dong.

Note: Other government bonds comprise government-guaranteed and municipal bonds.

Sources: Hanoi Stock Exchange, State Bank of Vietnam, Vietnam Bond Market Association, and Bloomberg LP.

Total LCY bond issuance rebounded in Q1 2025 on increased debt sales from the government and central bank. Overall issuance climbed 33.0% q-o-q to VND1,240.9 trillion in Q1 2025, reflecting a recovery from the previous quarter's 6.0% q-o-q contraction (**Figure 3**). Growth was buoyed by a substantial 88.1% q-o-q increase in government bond issuance, as the government ramped up its borrowing to foster economic growth amid global trade challenges. Additionally, issuance of central bank securities in open market operations rose 44.5% q-o-q to support the financial system. In contrast, corporate bond issuance fell 84.2% q-o-q in Q1 2025 due to a lack of participation by nonfinancial entities. During the

This market summary was written by Jeremy Grace Ilustrisimo, consultant, Economic Research and Development Impact Department, Asian Development Bank, Manila.

Figure 3: Composition of Local Currency Bond Issuance in Viet Nam

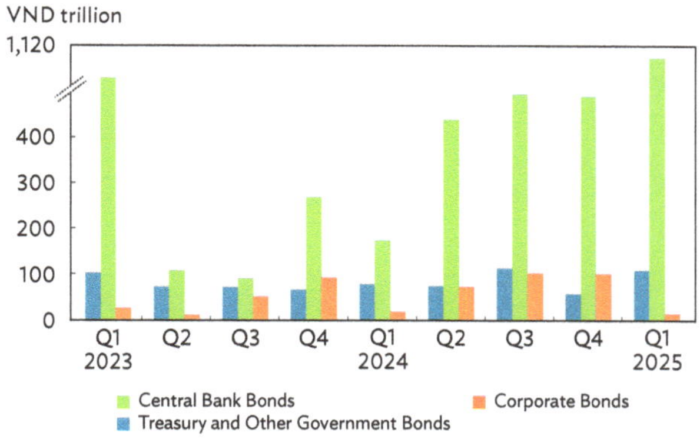

Q1 = first quarter, Q2 = second quarter, Q3 = third quarter, Q4 = fourth quarter, VND = Vietnamese dong.

Note: Other government bonds comprise government-guaranteed and municipal bonds.

Sources: Hanoi Stock Exchange, State Bank of Vietnam, Vietnam Bond Market Association, and Bloomberg LP.

quarter, the banking and finance sectors were the only issuers of LCY corporate bonds, accounting for 64.3% and 35.7%, respectively, of the corporate issuance total. VPS Securities issued the largest corporate bond in Q1 2025 with a debt sale of VND5.0 trillion, accounting for 30.8% of total corporate bond issuance during the quarter.

Investor Profile

Banks and insurance companies remained the two largest investor groups in the LCY government bond market. Collectively, these two dominant investor groups held 98.9% of LCY government bonds outstanding at the end of March, though this was down slightly from 99.5% a year earlier (**Figure 4**). Viet Nam had the highest Herfindahl–Hirschman Index score in emerging East Asia at the end of March, reflecting the least diversified investor holdings structure among its regional peers.[17]

Sustainable Bond Market

Viet Nam's sustainable bond market comprises green and sustainability instruments issued solely by the private sector. At the end of March, green and sustainability bonds accounted for 52.2% and 47.8%, respectively, of the total sustainable debt stock

Figure 4: Market Profile of the Two Dominant Investors for Local Currency Government Bonds

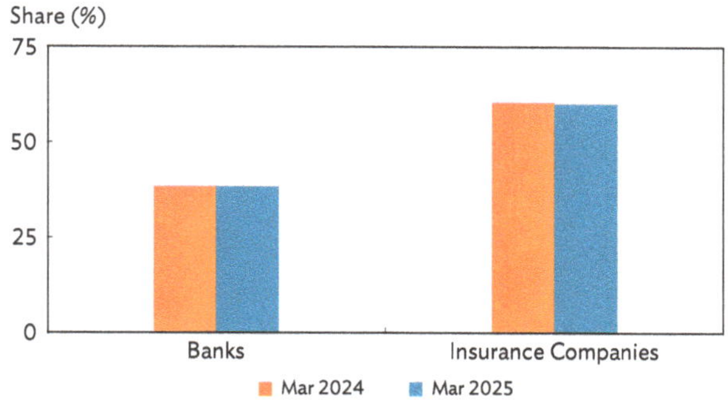

Source: Ministry of Finance, Viet Nam.

Figure 5: Market Profile of Outstanding Sustainable Bonds in Viet Nam at the End of March 2025

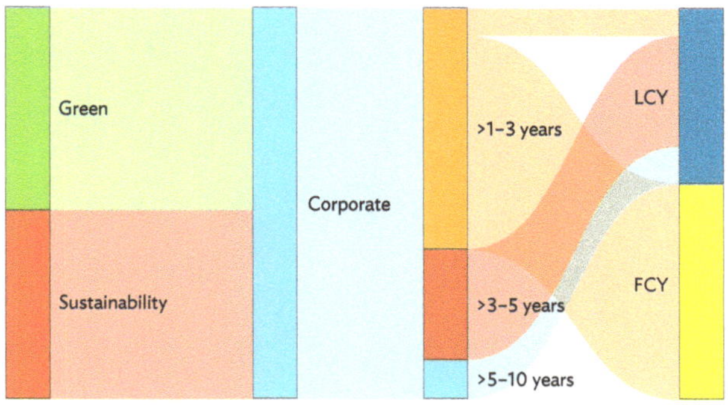

FCY = foreign currency, LCY = local currency.

Source: *AsianBondsOnline* calculations based on Bloomberg LP data.

(**Figure 5**). Total outstanding sustainable bonds reached USD1.1 billion in Q1 2025, making it one of the smallest sustainable bond markets in emerging East Asia, accounting for only 0.2% of the regional total. Foreign-currency-denominated sustainable bonds accounted for 54.8% of the total. Outstanding sustainable bonds were mainly concentrated in tenors of 1–3 years (61.7%) at the end of March. This led to a size-weighted average tenor of 2.7 years, among the shortest tenors across the region's sustainable bond markets.

[17] Emerging East Asia is defined to include member states of the Association of Southeast Asian Nations plus the People's Republic of China; Hong Kong, China; and the Republic of Korea. The Herfindahl–Hirschman Index is a common measure of market concentration. The index is used to measure the investor profile diversification of the local currency bond market by summing the squared share of each investor group in the bond market.

www.ingramcontent.com/pod-product-compliance
Lightning Source LLC
Chambersburg PA
CBHW041801220926
51847CB00014B/276
* 9 7 8 9 2 9 2 7 7 3 4 0 3 *